THE HEALING POWER OF TEARS

THE ART OF CRYING

PEPITA SANDWICH

VORACIOUS / LITTLE, BROWN AND COMPANY

HACHETTE BOOK GROUP

1290 AVENUE OF THE AMERICAS, NEW YORK, NY 10104

VORACIOUSBOOKS.COM

FIRST EDITION: APRIL 2024

VORACIOUS IS AN IMPRINT OF LITTLE, BROWN AND COMPANY, A DIVISION OF HACHETTE BOOK GROUP, INC. THE VORACIOUS NAME AND LOGO ARE TRADEMARKS OF HACHETTE BOOK GROUP, INC.

THE PUBLISHER IS NOT RESPONSIBLE FOR WEBSITES (OR THEIR CONTENT) THAT ARE NOT OWNED BY THE PUBLISHER.

THE HACHETTE SPEAKERS BUREAU PROVIDES A WIDE RANGE OF AUTHORS FOR SPEAKING EVENTS. TO FIND OUT MORE, GO TO HACHETTESPEAKERSBUREAU.COM OR CALL (866) 376-6591.

LITTLE, BROWN AND COMPANY BOOKS MAY BE PURCHASED IN BULK FOR BUSINESS, EDUCATIONAL, OR PROMOTIONAL USE.

FOR INFORMATION, PLEASE CONTACT YOUR LOCAL BOOKSELLER OR THE HACHETTE BOOK GROUP SPECIAL MARKETS DEPARTMENT AT SPECIAL.MARKETS@HBGUSA.COM.

ISBN 9780316532556

LCCN IS AVAILABLE AT THE LIBRARY OF CONGRESS

10 9 8 7 6 5 4 3 2 1

APS

PRINTED IN CHINA

CRYING DOES NOT INDICATE
THAT YOU ARE WEAK.
SINCE BIRTH, IT HAS ALWAYS
BEEN A SIGN THAT
YOU ARE ALIVE.
—CHARLOTTE BRONTË

✳ WHEN I FEEL ✳

LIKE MY BRAIN IS GOING TO MELT

THROUGH MY EARS AND THROUGH MY EYES

I TAKE A DEEP BREATH

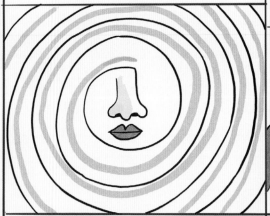

AND TRY TO INHALE EVERY MOLECULE OF OXYGEN IN THE ROOM

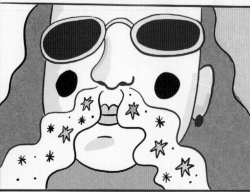

I CRY A LITTLE

AND MY MIND BECOMES CRYSTAL CLEAR.

TEARS INSIDE

CRYING CONTENTS

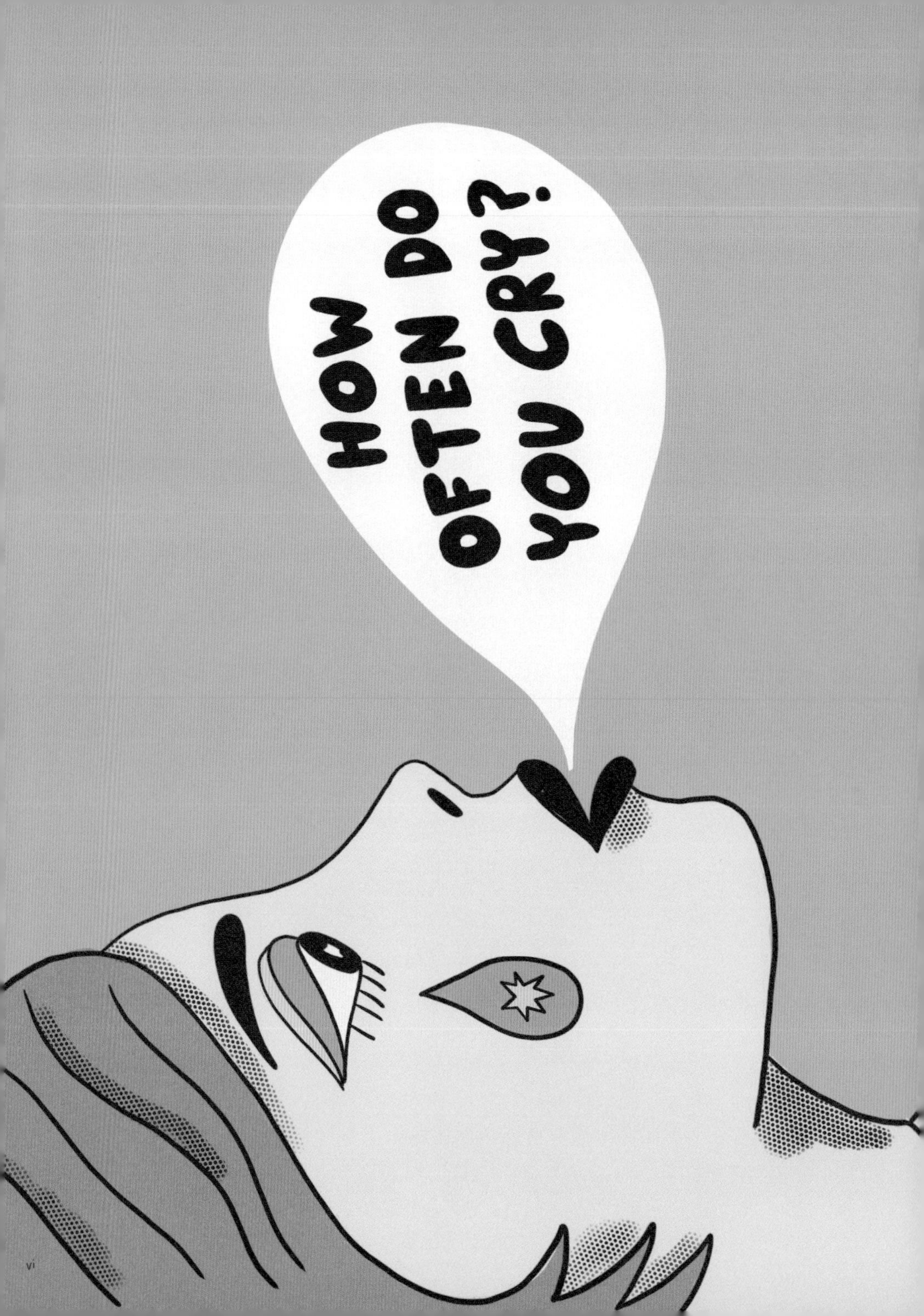
HOW OFTEN DO YOU CRY?

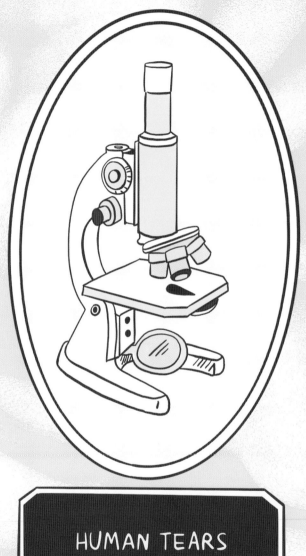

HUMAN TEARS

I HAVE ALWAYS CRIED A LOT. MY MOM SAYS I CRIED STEADILY, FROM THE MINUTE I WAS BORN UNTIL I TURNED NINE YEARS OLD. I WOULD CRY AT BUMPS, BRUISES, STRESSFUL SITUATIONS, AND MISUNDERSTANDINGS.

I CRY ALL THE TIME AND I USED TO FEEL SELF-CONSCIOUS ABOUT IT.

FOR YEARS, I WANTED TO CONTROL MY CRYING: I WOULD DO ANYTHING TO PREVENT TEARS FROM RUNNING DOWN MY FACE. I USED TO FEEL EMBARRASSED AND SCARED OF BEING PERCEIVED AS WEAK.

A FEW YEARS AGO, I MOVED FROM BUENOS AIRES TO NEW YORK CITY, AND AFTER HOURS AND HOURS OF CRYING INSIDE MY NEW EMPTY APARTMENT, I DECIDED TO START MY "CRYING DIARIES."

I WROTE DOWN AND DREW EVERY TIME I CRIED, AND IT HELPED ME FEEL MORE CONNECTED TO MY TEARS.

RESEARCH HAS FOUND THAT IN ADDITION TO BEING SELF-SOOTHING, SHEDDING EMOTIONAL TEARS RELEASES OXYTOCIN AND ENDORPHINS. THESE CHEMICALS MAKE YOU FEEL GOOD.

IN THE PAST, CRYING MY HEART OUT HELPED ME GET THROUGH DIFFICULT AND UNPREDICTABLE TIMES.

CHARLES DARWIN ONCE DECLARED EMOTIONAL TEARS "PURPOSELESS."

CRYING STILL REMAINS LARGELY TABOO IN SOCIETY.

WHY IS CRYING CONSIDERED A BAD THING? WHAT DOES IT MEAN IF WE CRY, AND WHY DO WE SO OFTEN TRY TO HIDE OUR TEARS?

CRYING IS SPECIAL. HUMANS ARE THE ONLY CREATURES WHOSE TEARS CAN BE TRIGGERED BY THEIR FEELINGS.

CRYING IS ONE OF THE MOST BEAUTIFUL FORMS OF BODILY EXPRESSION.

WE CRY BECAUSE WE NEED OTHER PEOPLE, BECAUSE WE FEEL EMOTIONS DEEPLY, BECAUSE WE'RE ALIVE.

CRYING IS COMPLETELY NORMAL.

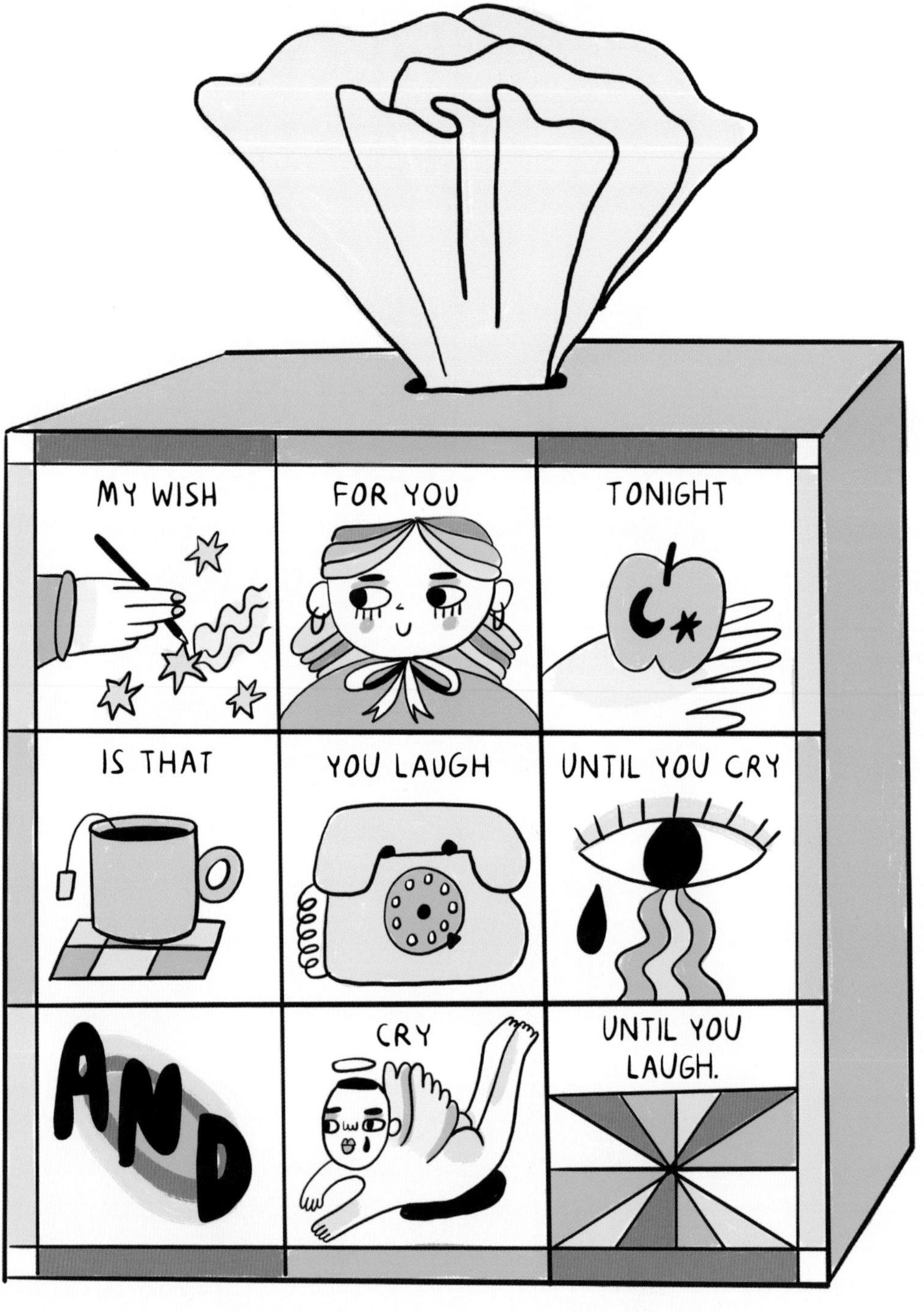
MY WISH
FOR YOU
TONIGHT
IS THAT
YOU LAUGH
UNTIL YOU CRY
AND
CRY
UNTIL YOU LAUGH.

THE SCIENCE OF CRYING

THERE ARE THREE TYPES OF TEARS.

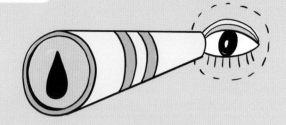

BASAL TEARS: THESE TEARS KEEP THE EYES LUBRICATED. THEY MAKE VISION AS WE KNOW IT POSSIBLE BY SMOOTHING OUT THE IRREGULARITIES OF THE EYE. TEARY EYES HELP US SEE THE WORLD.

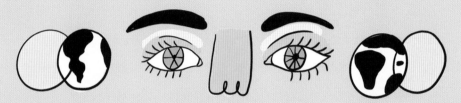

REFLEX TEARS: THESE RESULT FROM IRRITATION OF THE EYES, THE BODY'S WAY OF WASHING OUT FOREIGN PARTICLES. THEY CAN ALSO APPEAR FROM EXPERIENCING TOO-BRIGHT LIGHT OR HOT OR SPICY STIMULI TO THE TONGUE AND MOUTH. REFLEX TEARS ARE ALSO LINKED WITH VOMITING, COUGHING, AND YAWNING.

EMOTIONAL TEARS: THESE TEARS BURST FORTH IN RESPONSE TO STRONG EMOTIONS, LIKE SADNESS, GRIEF, JOY, OR RAGE. MOST RESEARCHERS BELIEVE THAT EMOTIONAL TEARS ARE UNIQUE TO HUMANS.

11

TEARS ARE SALTY BECAUSE OF ELECTROLYTES, ALSO KNOWN AS SALT IONS. OUR BODY PRODUCES ELECTROLYTES TO CREATE THE ENERGY THAT HELPS OUR BRAIN FUNCTION AND OUR MUSCLES MOVE. TEARS ARE COMPOSED OF WATER, SALTS, ANTIBODIES, AND LYSOZYMES (ANTIBACTERIAL ENZYMES). HOWEVER, THESE COMPOSITIONS VARY AMONG THE DIFFERENT TEAR TYPES.

EMOTIONAL TEARS HAVE THE SAME CHEMICAL COMPONENTS AS BASAL TEARS BUT CONTAIN HIGHER CONCENTRATIONS OF STRESS HORMONES AND NATURAL PAIN KILLERS, WHICH SUGGESTS THAT EMOTIONAL TEARS HAVE A BIOLOGICAL ROLE IN BALANCING STRESS HORMONE LEVELS.

CARL SAGAN ONCE SAID THAT HUMANS ARE MADE OF STAR STUFF.

FINDING OUR PLACE IN THE COSMOS CAN BE SOUL-STIRRING.

EVERY TIME I LOOK AT THE MOON, ON A CLEAR NIGHT, I AM DEEPLY MOVED AND CRY.

 WEDNESDAY, SEPTEMBER 2ND, 2020. I CRIED AND FELL ASLEEP, FULL MOON IN PISCES.

WHAT HAPPENS IN THE BODY WHEN YOU CRY

YOU FEEL A POWERFUL EMOTION AND THE AMYGDALA SENDS A SIGNAL TO THE HYPOTHALAMUS, A SMALL REGION IN YOUR BRAIN THAT'S CONNECTED TO YOUR AUTONOMIC NERVOUS SYSTEM.

THE NERVOUS SYSTEM ACCELERATES THE FIGHT-OR-FLIGHT RESPONSE, WHICH TRIES TO PROTECT YOU BY STOPPING YOU FROM PERFORMING ANY NORMAL FUNCTIONS, LIKE EATING OR DRINKING. AS A RESULT, YOU FEEL A LUMP IN THE THROAT.

WITH YOUR BODY FULLY ALERTED, YOU ALSO EXPERIENCE OTHER SYMPTOMS ASSOCIATED WITH SHOCK. YOUR HEART RATE MIGHT INCREASE, YOUR LIPS START TO QUIVER, AND YOUR VOICE GETS SHAKY.

ALL THESE FEELINGS TELL YOUR HYPOTHALAMUS TO PRODUCE A CHEMICAL MESSENGER CALLED ACETYLCHOLINE, WHICH BINDS TO RECEPTORS IN YOUR BRAIN THAT SEND SIGNALS TO THE LACHRYMAL GLANDS TO START PRODUCING TEARS.

THE EYES FILL UP PRETTY QUICKLY, AND THE TEARS START ROLLING DOWN YOUR FACE. TEARS WILL ALSO START TO FLOOD YOUR NASAL CAVITY AND COME OUT OF YOUR NOSE. YOUR EYEBROWS RISE, YOUR EYELIDS DROP, AND THE CORNERS OF YOUR MOUTH LOWER.

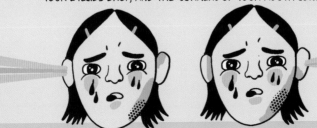

WHEN EVERYTHING IS OVER, YOU USUALLY FEEL MUCH BETTER THAN JUST BEFORE CRYING.

CRYING IS THE RESULT OF A FASCINATING CHAIN REACTION IN THE BODY. HUMAN NEWBORN BABIES DO NOT HAVE FULLY DEVELOPED LACHRYMAL GLANDS AND CAN'T PRODUCE VISIBLE TEARS BUT STILL FROWN AND CRY LOUDLY TO ASK FOR LOVE OR ASSISTANCE. USUALLY, BABIES START SHEDDING REALLY VISIBLE TEARS SOMETIME BETWEEN ONE AND THREE MONTHS OF AGE.

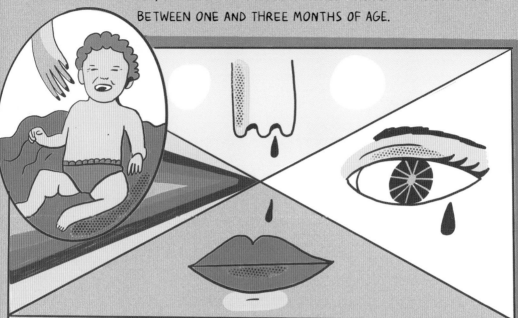

FROM BIRTH WE CRY BECAUSE WE NEED OTHERS.

TEARS PROTECT US FROM THE WORLD.

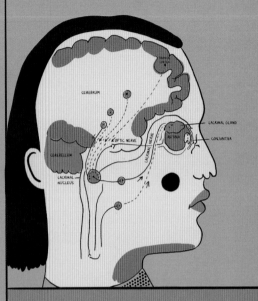

BASAL TEARS FORM A PERMEABLE BARRIER THAT PRESERVES THE EYES.

EMOTIONAL TEARS

ARE THE CUSTODIANS OF THE HEART.

THE FASCINATING THING ABOUT EMOTIONAL CRYING, IS THAT YOU CAN BREAK INTO TEARS EVEN WHEN YOU ARE HAPPY.

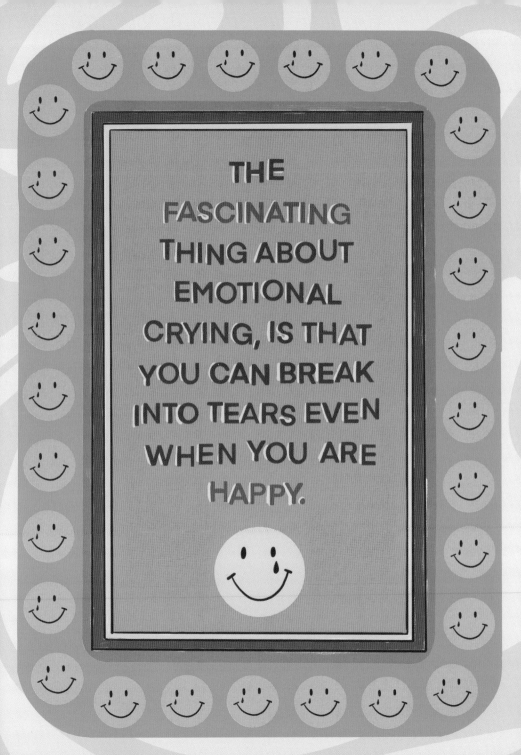

WHEN I VISITED IGUAZÚ FALLS IN ARGENTINA, AND I REACHED LA GARGANTA DEL DIABLO (THE DEVIL'S THROAT)—ONE OF THE LARGEST WATERFALLS IN THE WORLD—I CRIED BECAUSE I DIDN'T KNOW HOW ELSE TO EXPRESS MY JOY AT WITNESSING SUCH A FASCINATING WATER SPECTACLE FROM NATURE.

SHEDDING TEARS INSIDE THE MIST OF THESE COSMIC WATERFALLS, WHILE BEING SURROUNDED BY THE ROARING SOUNDS OF POWERFUL CASCADES, FELT MORE TO ME LIKE HEAVEN THAN LIKE BEING INSIDE AN EVIL SPIRIT'S MOUTH.

CRYING TEARS OF JOY MAY BE THE BODY'S WAY OF RESTORING EMOTIONAL EQUILIBRIUM. RESPONDING TO AN OVERWHELMINGLY POSITIVE EMOTION WITH A PHYSICAL RELEASE HELPS US RECOVER BETTER FROM POWERFUL FEELINGS.

THROUGH CHILDHOOD AND EARLY ADOLESCENCE, PHYSICAL PAIN LIKE SCRAPES AND BRUISES ARE ALSO COMMON TRIGGERS FOR EMOTIONAL TEARS. THESE INJURY-RELATED EMOTIONAL TEARS TEND TO DECREASE AS WE BECOME ADULTS.

AS WE TRANSITION INTO ADULTHOOD, EMOTIONAL TEARS ARE TRIGGERED BY A BROADER RANGE OF FEELINGS THAT INCLUDE: ATTACHMENT-RELATED PAIN; COMPASSIONATE PAIN; SOCIETAL PAIN; AND NOSTALGIC, SENTIMENTAL, OR MORAL FEELINGS.

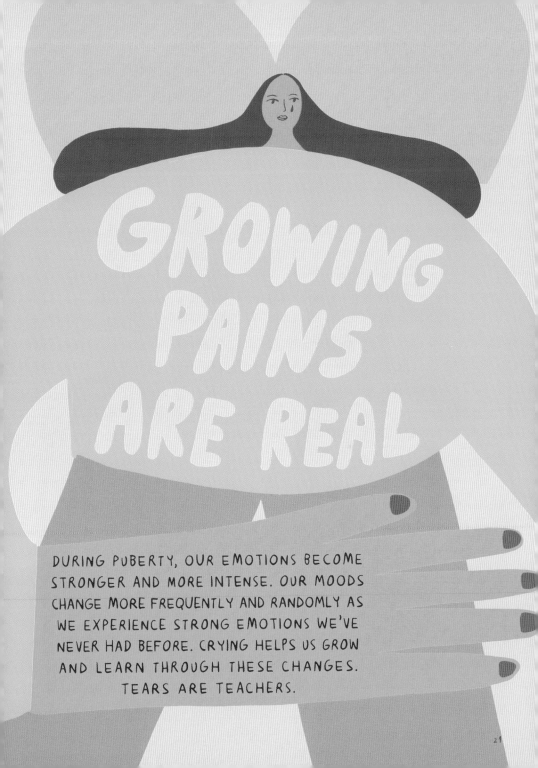

GROWING PAINS ARE REAL

DURING PUBERTY, OUR EMOTIONS BECOME STRONGER AND MORE INTENSE. OUR MOODS CHANGE MORE FREQUENTLY AND RANDOMLY AS WE EXPERIENCE STRONG EMOTIONS WE'VE NEVER HAD BEFORE. CRYING HELPS US GROW AND LEARN THROUGH THESE CHANGES. TEARS ARE TEACHERS.

WHEN MY YOUNGER BROTHER, JAVIER, BROKE UP WITH HIS FIRST
GIRLFRIEND, I WAS FIFTEEN AND HE WAS THIRTEEN. I REMEMBER WATCHING
HIM CRY IN BED FOR DAYS. AT ONE POINT, I SAT DOWN IN HIS ROOM AND,
WITHOUT SAYING A WORD, STARTED SHEDDING TEARS WITH HIM. I FELT HIS
PAIN, AND WE BEGAN A TELEPATHIC DANCE OF TEARS. AFTER A WHILE, HE
FELT BETTER AND THANKED ME FOR CRYING BY HIS SIDE.

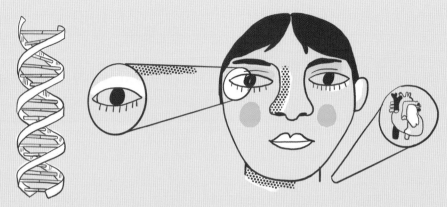

CRYING IS ASSOCIATED WITH THE PARASYMPATHETIC NERVOUS SYSTEM, WHICH SOOTHES THE MIND AND BODY. BEING ABLE TO CRY EMOTIONALLY AND RESPONDING TO THAT PHYSICAL EXPRESSION IN OTHERS IS A FUNDAMENTAL PART OF THE HUMAN CONDITION.

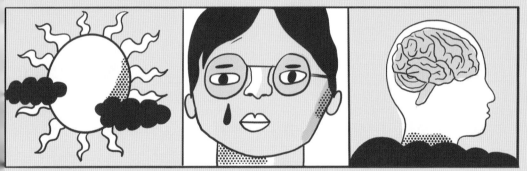

SEEING SOMEONE ELSE IN TEARS ACTIVATES THE SAME NEURONAL AREAS OF THE BRAIN THAT ARE ACTIVATED BY BEING IN THE CRYING STATE ONESELF. THERE MUST HAVE BEEN SOME POINT IN OUR HUMAN EVOLUTION WHEN TEARS CAME TO TRIGGER EMPATHY AND COMPASSION.

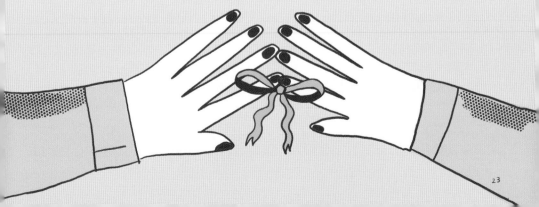

IN 1906, ALVIN BORGQUIST, A WHITE GRADUATE STUDENT AT CLARK UNIVERSITY, PUBLISHED THE WORLD'S FIRST THOROUGH PSYCHOLOGICAL STUDY OF CRYING. THE RESULTS OF HIS INVESTIGATION ARE WEIRD AND FULL OF RACIAL ASSUMPTIONS. FOR HIS RESEARCH, HE WANTED TO KNOW WHETHER OR NOT BLACK PEOPLE CRIED AND CREATED A QUESTIONNAIRE TO GATHER DATA ON TYPICAL CRYING BEHAVIORS THAT BEGAN LIKE THIS:

AS A CHILD DID YOU EVER CRY TILL YOU ALMOST LOST CONSCIOUSNESS OR THINGS SEEMED TO CHANGE ABOUT YOU? DESCRIBE A CRY WITH UTTER ABANDON. DID IT BRING A SENSE OF UTTER DESPAIR?

DESCRIBE AS FULLY AS YOU CAN SUCH AN EXPERIENCE IN YOURSELF, YOUR SUBJECTIVE FEELINGS, HOW IT GREW, WHAT CAUSED AND INCREASED IT, ITS PHYSICAL SYMPTOMS, AND ALL ITS AFTEREFFECTS. WHAT IS WANTED IS A PICTURE OF A GENUINE AND UNFORCED FIT OR CRISIS OF PURE MISERY.

BORGQUIST WROTE THESE QUESTIONS IN A LETTER TO W. E. B. DU BOIS, A SCHOLAR AND THE FIRST AFRICAN AMERICAN PHD FROM HARVARD UNIVERSITY. BORGQUIST WAS A COLLEGE-EDUCATED WHITE PERSON WHO LIVED SUCH AN ISOLATED EXISTENCE THAT HE DIDN'T EVEN KNOW IF BLACK PEOPLE WERE CAPABLE OF CRYING, AND THAT MAKES ME CRY.

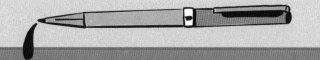

MY OWN CRYING QUESTIONNAIRE

WHEN WAS THE LAST TIME YOU CRIED?

WHAT'S YOUR FIRST CRYING MEMORY?

DO YOU PREFER CRYING BY YOURSELF OR AROUND LOVED ONES?

DO YOU ENJOY TAKING A NAP AFTER CRYING OR WOULD YOU RATHER TAKE A WALK?

WHAT IS YOUR FAVORITE PLACE TO CRY?

WOULD YOU DRINK THE TEARS OF SOMEONE YOU LOVE?

WHAT MOVIE ALWAYS MAKES YOU CRY?

ARE YOU MOVED TO TEARS WHEN YOU SEE SOMEONE CRY?

IN 1872, CHARLES DARWIN WROTE HIS THIRD MAJOR WORK ON EVOLUTION CALLED *THE EXPRESSION OF EMOTIONS IN MAN AND ANIMALS.* HE CONCLUDED THAT WE EXPRESS EMOTION IN ORDER TO REDUCE DISTRESS.

DARWIN CAME TO BELIEVE THAT CRYING HAD SOME EVOLUTIONARY ADVANTAGES. FOR EXAMPLE, BABIES CAN COMMUNICATE BY CRYING WHEN THEY ARE HUNGRY. HE THEORIZED THAT TEARS ARE SIMPLY THE SIDE EFFECTS OF CALLING FOR HELP. BUT HE WAS NOT ABLE TO EXPLAIN WHY SOMETIMES WE SILENTLY CRY IN RESPONSE TO SADNESS OR BEAUTY. HE HYPOTHESIZED THAT TEARS ARE DUE TO HABIT: WE CRY BECAUSE OF AN EMOTIONAL PATTERN WE DEVELOP IN EARLY CHILDHOOD.

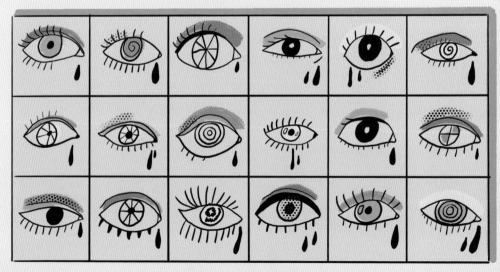

WHEN YOU EXPERIENCE A POWERFUL FEELING AND THE SIGNALS IN YOUR BRAIN START TO LIGHT UP, IT FEELS LIKE YOUR WHOLE BODY CAN EXPRESS WHAT YOU ARE EXPERIENCING. TO FEEL A STRONG EMOTION AND CRY IS TO ACKNOWLEDGE YOUR MIND THROUGH YOUR PHYSICAL BODY.

SOME THEORISTS SAY THAT CRYING MAY HAVE EVOLVED AS A KIND OF SIGNAL—
A BODY LANGUAGE THAT IS IMPORTANT BECAUSE IT CAN ONLY BE PICKED UP
BY PEOPLE CLOSE TO US WHO CAN ACTUALLY SEE OUR TEARS. TEARS LET OUR
INTIMATES IN—PEOPLE NEAR US, WHO WOULD BE MORE LIKELY TO SUPPORT AND
GUARD US.

 FRIDAY, OCTOBER 29TH, 2021. I CRIED AT A HALLOWEEN
PARTY. THE THEME WAS STUDIO 54.

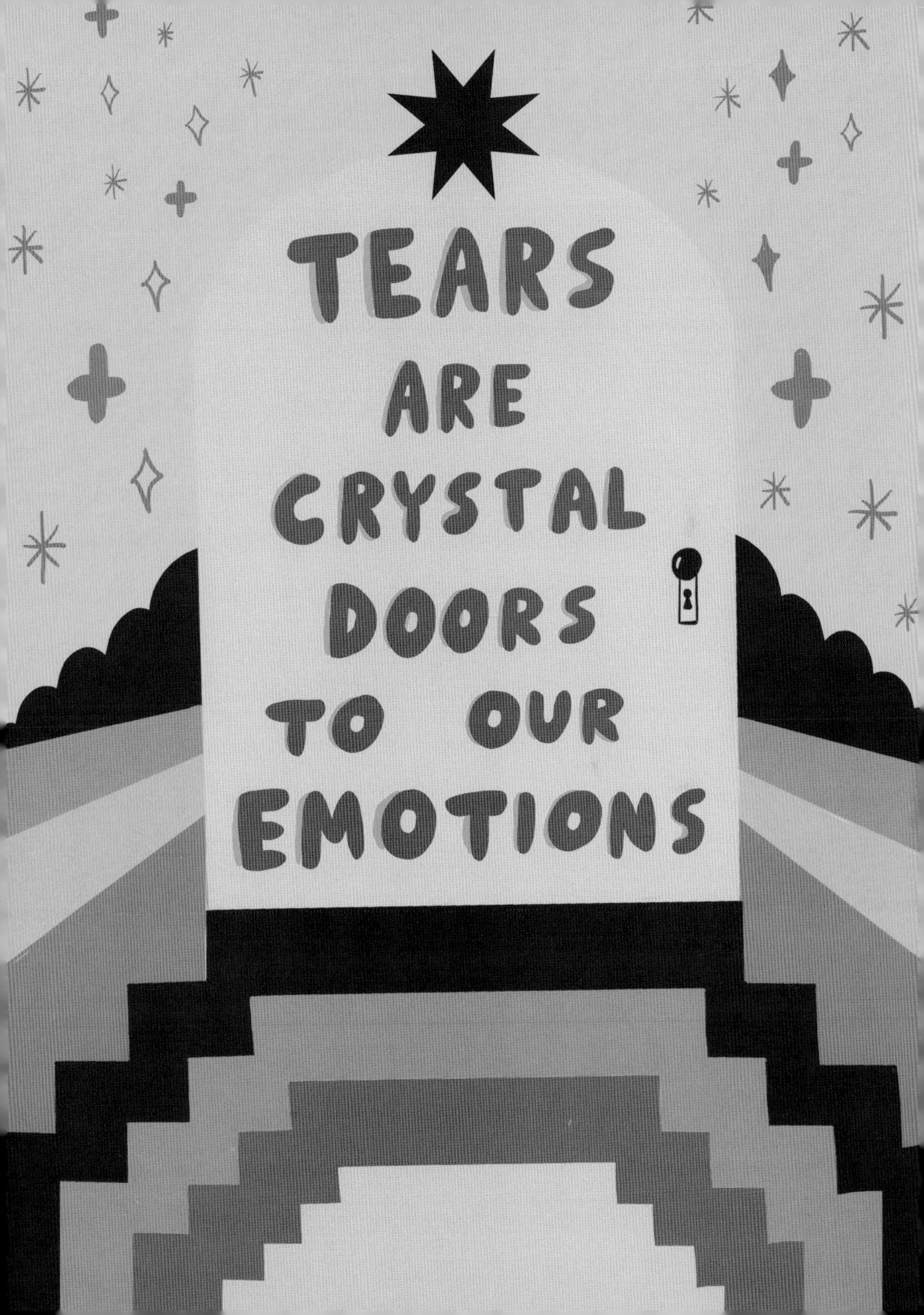
TEARS
ARE
CRYSTAL
DOORS
TO OUR
EMOTIONS

WE KNOW SO LITTLE ABOUT THE HUMAN BRAIN THAT DURING THE 1960S A
BOLD HYPOTHESIS SUGGESTED HUMANS EVOLVED FROM AQUATIC APES
AND AT ONE POINT TEARS HELPED US SURVIVE IN SALT WATER.

THIS CONTROVERSIAL HYPOTHESIS OF HUMAN EVOLUTION

POSTULATES THAT THE ANCESTORS OF MODERN HUMANS TOOK A DIFFERENT EVOLUTIONARY PATH

AND BECAME ADAPTED TO A MORE AQUATIC HOME.

 TUESDAY, JANUARY 10TH, 2023. I CRIED THINKING ABOUT
THE FIRST HUMANS TO INHABIT THE PLANET.

ALTHOUGH THE INVESTIGATION OF THE HUMAN BRAIN HAS MANY UNSOLVED MYSTERIES, MOUNTING EVIDENCE SUPPORTS MORE PROBABLE THEORIES. ONE IS THAT TEARS MOTIVATE BONDING AND HUMAN CONNECTION. WHILE MOST OTHER ANIMALS ARE BORN FULLY FORMED, HUMANS COME INTO THIS WORLD PHYSICALLY UNEQUIPPED TO DEAL WITH LIFE ON THEIR OWN. HUMAN INFANTS ARE ESPECIALLY VULNERABLE BECAUSE THEIR BRAINS ARE LESS DEVELOPED IN COMPARISON TO THE YOUNG OF OTHER SPECIES.

ANTHROPOLOGISTS HAVE LONG THOUGHT THAT THE REDUCTION OF THE PELVIS, WHICH MADE WALKING ON TWO LEGS POSSIBLE, HAS LIMITED HUMAN GESTATION LENGTH. SOME SCIENTISTS ALSO BELIEVE THAT THE TIMING OF HUMAN BIRTH ACTUALLY OPTIMIZES COGNITIVE AND MOTOR NEURONAL DEVELOPMENT OUTSIDE IN THE WORLD.

"MAYBE HUMAN NEWBORNS ARE ADAPTED TO SOAKING UP ALL THIS CULTURAL STUFF AND MAYBE BEING BORN EARLIER LETS YOU DO THIS," STATED ADOLF PORTMANN, SWISS ZOOLOGIST.

EMOTIONAL CRYING OFTEN TELLS OTHER PEOPLE THAT YOU ARE IN SOME SITUATION THAT IS, AT LEAST IN THAT PRECISE MOMENT, BEYOND YOUR COPING ABILITIES.

BUT TEARS CAN ALSO BE A KIND OF ACTIVE SIGNAL

TO YOURSELF

THAT THERE IS SOMETHING IMPORTANT

HAPPENING INSIDE YOUR BRAIN.

CRYING IS A SPECIAL PSYCHIC CALL FOR HELP
AND CONNECTION.

WHILE THERE ARE STILL UNANSWERED ISSUES IN THE ENIGMATIC STUDY OF EMOTIONAL TEARS, WE ARE CERTAIN THAT FEELINGS CHANGE AND DEVELOP THROUGHOUT OUR WHOLE LIVES AS WE AGE AND MAKE OUR WAY FROM CHILDHOOD TO ADULTHOOD.

SOME BIG QUESTIONS STILL REMAIN: HOW MUCH OF OUR CRYING IS BIOLOGICAL AND HOW MUCH SOCIETAL? IS IT OUR DEEP HUMAN EMOTIONS THAT EVOLVE OR OUR ABILITY TO COPE WITH AND CONTROL OUR TEARS?

THE CRYING
WHEEL OF FORTUNE

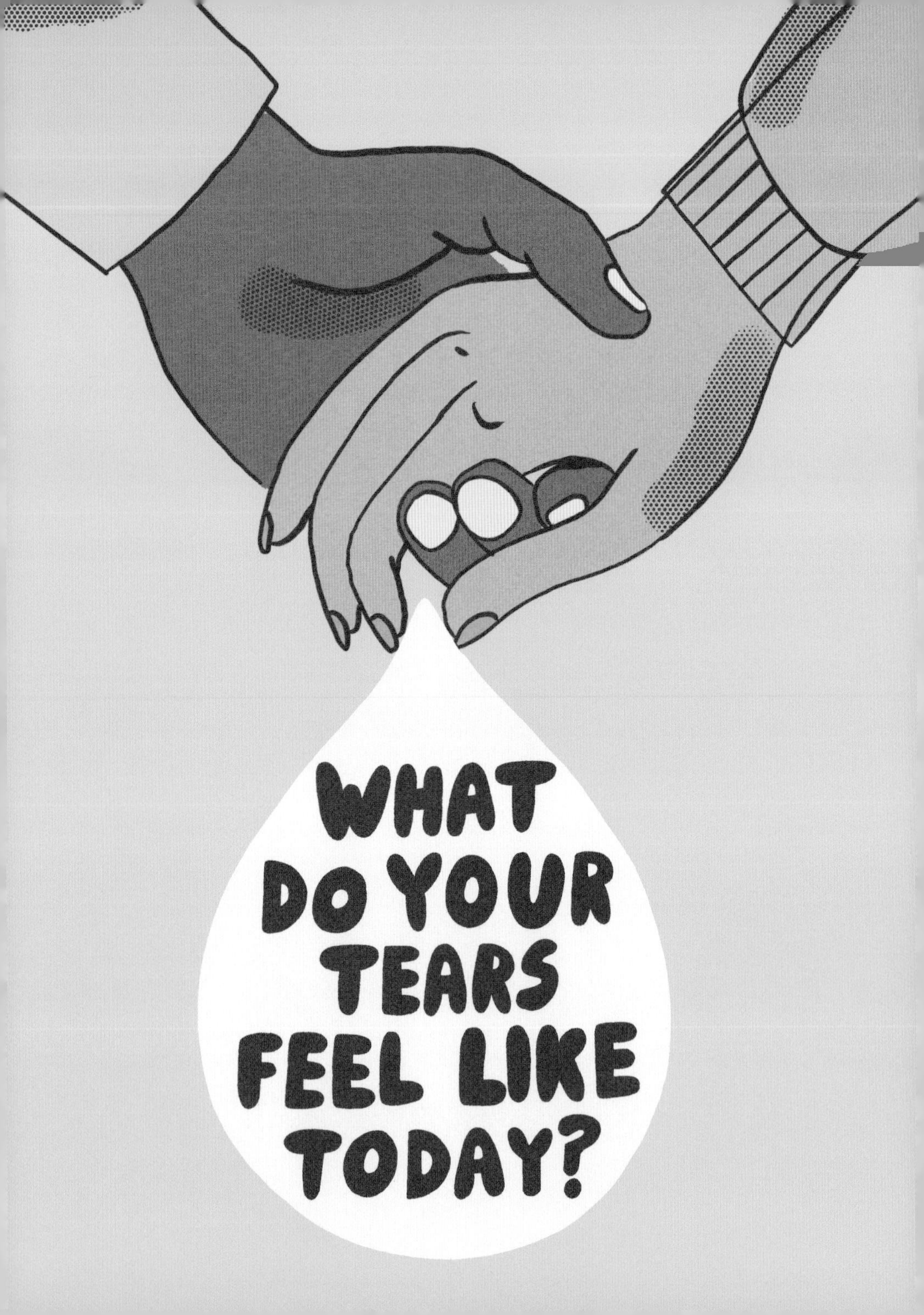
WHAT DO YOUR TEARS FEEL LIKE TODAY?

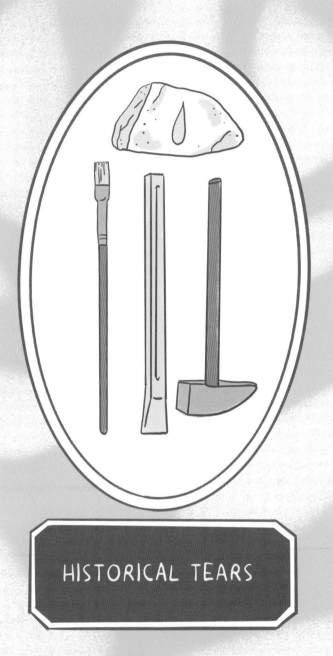

HISTORICAL TEARS

MY EARLIEST CRYING MEMORY IS FROM 1988. I WAS TWO YEARS OLD, MY
MOM WAS PREGNANT, AND I REALLY WANTED A BABY SISTER. WHEN SHE
FINALLY TOLD ME I WAS GOING TO HAVE A BROTHER, I CRIED FOR TWO
DAYS. I FEEL LIKE I CAN REMEMBER THE SENSE OF DISAPPOINTMENT.
I WAS GRIEVING A POSSIBILITY.

NOW EVERYTHING HAS CHANGED AND THOSE PARTICULAR TEARS FROM THE
PAST FEEL IRRELEVANT. I LOVE MY BROTHER AND, LIKE MANY OTHER ASPECTS
OF MY LIFE, MY CRYING REASONS HAVE MUTATED AND EVOLVED.

HUMANS HAVE BEEN COMMUNICATING EMOTIONS SINCE THE BEGINNING OF OUR EXISTENCE.

THE PAST, THE PRESENT, AND THE FUTURE ARE CONNECTED BY PSYCHIC TEARS.

PSYCHOLOGISTS FROM ULM UNIVERSITY IN GERMANY AND UNIVERSITY OF SUSSEX IN ENGLAND BELIEVED EMOTIONAL TEARS OCCURRED WHEN BASIC PSYCHOLOGICAL NEEDS WERE EITHER NOT SATISFIED OR VERY INTENSIVELY ACHIEVED. THEY BROKE DOWN HUMAN TEARS INTO FIVE CATEGORIES.

LONELINESS

POWERLESSNESS

EXCESSIVE DEMANDS

HARMONY

MEDIA CONSUMPTION

OUR ANCESTORS FELT EMOTION. EMOTIONAL TEARS MIGHT HAVE A PREHISTORIC MEANING. HAPPINESS, SADNESS, FEAR, AND ANGER ARE CONSIDERED PRIMITIVE FEELINGS.

 MONDAY, APRIL 6TH, 2020. MY PHONE MADE A VIDEO WITH MEMORIES FROM TWO YEARS EARLIER, AND I STARTED CRYING.

EVOLUTIONARY SCIENTISTS BELIEVE THAT HUMANS DEVELOPED EMOTIONAL CRYING TO SERVE A SOCIAL FUNCTION. THESE EXPERTS SUGGEST THAT CRYING PROVIDES A VISUAL AND AUDITORY SIGNAL TO OTHER PEOPLE, AND LETS THEM KNOW THAT YOU ARE IN NEED OF SOCIAL SUPPORT AND NURTURING. SINCE THE BEGINNING OF HUMAN HISTORY, WE HAVE FEARED ABANDONMENT AND NEVER WANTED TO FEEL LONELINESS.

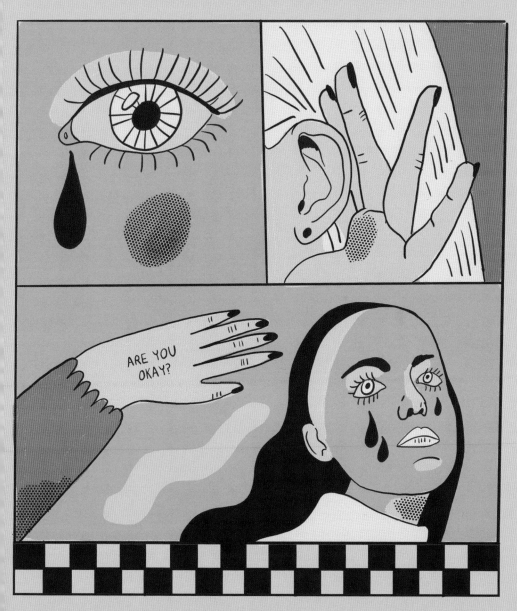

TEARS OF GODS

IN ACCORDANCE WITH ANCIENT EGYPTIAN MYTHOLOGY, WHEN THE SUN GOD RE CRIED, HIS TEARS TRANSFORMED INTO HONEYBEES AFTER TOUCHING THE GROUND. THUS THE HONEYBEE WAS SACRED IN ANCIENT EGYPTIAN CULTURE. THESE TEARS WERE SPECIAL AND TOOK ON CULTURAL IMPORTANCE IN EVERYTHING FROM TRADE TO DEATH RITUALS.

 TUESDAY, DECEMBER 1ST, 2020. I CRIED IN THE MUSEUM TRYING TO COMMUNICATE TELEPATHICALLY WITH AN EGYPTIAN SCULPTURE FROM THE TEMPLE OF DENDUR.

THE NILE RIVER WAS ANOTHER SOURCE OF GREAT MYTHOLOGY FOR ANCIENT EGYPTIANS. THEY BELIEVED THAT THE NILE FLOODED DUE TO THE TEARS OF ISIS—THE GODDESS OF FERTILITY—WHILE SHE MOURNED THE DEATH OF HER BELOVED HUSBAND, OSIRIS. THE FLOODING OF THE NILE IS AN IMPORTANT NATURAL CYCLE, AND EGYPTIANS STILL CELEBRATE NILE FLOOD DAY, THANKING THEIR RIVER FOR ITS LOYALTY WITH FLOWERS, SONGS, AND DANCES.

A PORTAL

TO CRY

TELEPATHIC TEARS

THAT TAKE ME BACK

TO ANCIENT GALAXIES.

43

THE AZTECS OFTEN SOBBED AND PRACTICED "RITUAL WEEPING."
IT WAS COMMON FOR AZTECS TO CRY FREELY WHEN GIVING THANKS FOR
SOMETHING SPECIAL, LIKE THE GRANTING OF LAND TO A FAMILY.
INDIVIDUAL TEARS SHED BY CHILDREN IN PARTICULAR WERE POWERFUL
SYMBOLS FOR RAIN. THEY SERVED AS A FORM OF EXCHANGE WHEN
OFFERED TO THE RAIN GOD TLALOC DURING THE FARMING AND
FESTIVE TIMES OF THE YEAR. IT WAS CONSIDERED A GOOD OMEN IF
INFANTS SACRIFICED FOR TLALOC WERE CRYING
THEIR HEARTS OUT AT THESE RITUALS.

TUESDAY, JULY 5TH, 2022. I CRIED IN TEOTIHUACÁN, MEXICO, VISITING
THE SUN AND THE MOON PYRAMIDS.

Crying Moon

GOLD AND SILVER WERE ESSENTIAL ELEMENTS AND POWERFUL SYMBOLS LINKING THE INCAS TO THE COSMOS. GOLD WAS CONNECTED TO THE SUN, ALSO KNOWN IN THE INCA WORLD AS THE "SWEAT OF THE SUN." THE SUN'S WIFE WAS "MOTHER MOON" AND WAS REPRESENTED BY SILVER BECAUSE THIS ELEMENT WAS THOUGHT TO COME FROM THE MOON'S TEARS.

WEEPING AND WAILING PERFORMANCES IN CHINESE ANTIQUITY WERE ASSOCIATED WITH MOURNING FOR THE DEAD, PROTESTING, AND CALMING THE SPIRITS. MORE THAN JUST A REBELLIOUS RUSH OF GRIEF, THE "PERFORMANCE" OF CRYING—CALLED *KU*—COULD BE APPRECIATED FOR ITS AESTHETIC AND ENTERTAINING ATTRIBUTES.

APART FROM WAILING AT FUNERALS, THE TERM *KU* WAS ALSO USED IN ANCIENT TIMES TO REFER TO A PUBLIC ACT INVOLVING THE CHANTING AND DRAMATIC ENACTMENT OF DEEP HUMAN EMOTION.

THE SINCERITY OF TEARS HAS BEEN CRUCIAL FOR MANY RELIGIONS AND CULTURES, EITHER IN PRIVATE PRAYERS OR IN LARGE GROUP RITUALS.

IN JERUSALEM, THE WAILING WALL IS A POWERFUL AND ENERGETIC PLACE FOR DIVINE DEVOTION WHERE TEARS ARE VALUED AND EXPECTED.

DURING THE ANNUAL ISLAMIC PILGRIMAGE TO MECCA (HAJJ), CRIERS CALLED THE WEEPING SUFIS SHED TEARS THAT ARE CONSIDERED A SIGN OF THE GENUINENESS OF THEIR MYSTICAL EXPERIENCE.

TEARS STARTED HAVING SUCH A SPECIAL KIND OF POWER, AS A SEAL OF AUTHENTIC FAITH, THAT EVEN RELIGIOUS STATUES ARE BELIEVED TO SHED TEARS.

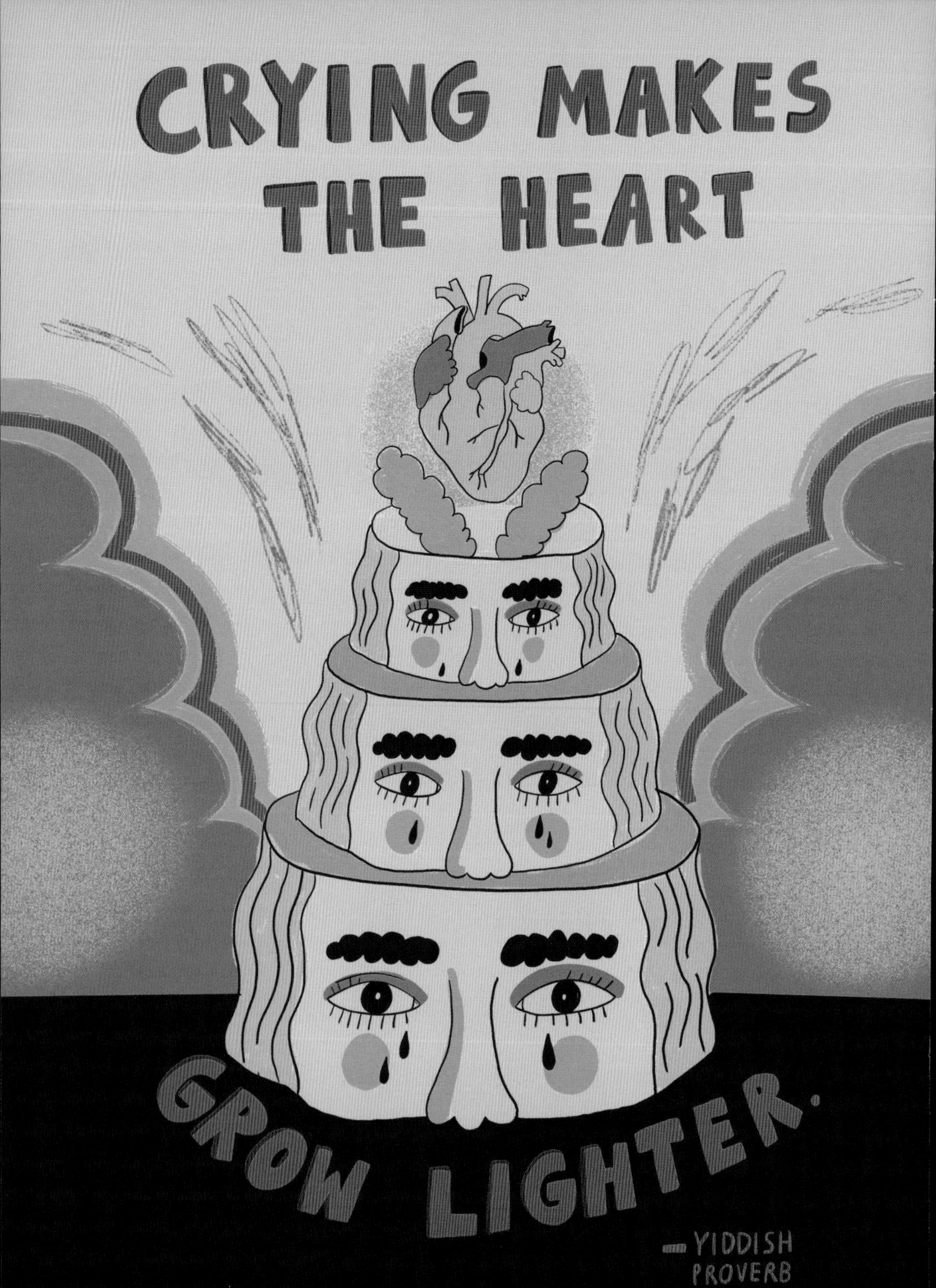
CRYING MAKES
THE HEART
GROW LIGHTER.
—YIDDISH
PROVERB

CRYING STUDIES

PEOPLE HAVE BEEN RESEARCHING THE ORIGIN OF TEARS, AND WHY HUMANS DEVELOPED A CRYING RESPONSE, SINCE ABOUT 1500 BCE. FOR A LONG TIME, IT WAS THOUGHT THAT TEARS WERE MADE INSIDE THE HEART. IN THE OLD TESTAMENT, TEARS ARE DESCRIBED AS THE CONSEQUENCE OF THE PUMPING HEART DISSOLVING INTO WATER THAT CAME OUT FROM THE EYES.

DURING THE CLASSICAL GREEK PERIOD, HIPPOCRATES THOUGHT THAT THE MIND WAS THE TRIGGER FOR TEARS. HE ACCORDINGLY DESCRIBED TEARS AS "THE HUMORS FROM THE BRAIN." FOR HIPPOCRATIC DOCTORS, ONE OF THE MOST EFFECTIVE CURES FOR BODY FLUID IMBALANCE WAS PURGING THROUGH CRYING.

FROM THE GREEK *KATHARSIS*, "CATHARSIS" IS AN EMOTIONAL RELEASE THAT PROVIDES RENEWAL AND RESTORATION. THE WORD WAS USED BY ARISTOTLE IN *POETICS*, IN WHICH HE COMPARED THE EFFECTS OF TRAGEDY ON THE MIND OF A SPECTATOR TO ITS EFFECTS ON THE BODY. IN PSYCHOLOGY, THE TERM IS ASSOCIATED WITH FREUDIAN PSYCHOANALYSIS AND IS SPECIFICALLY RELATED TO THE EXPRESSION OF BURIED TRAUMA. WHEN CATHARSIS IS SUCCESSFUL, IT BRINGS TRAUMA INTO CONSCIOUSNESS, THUS ERASING IT, WHICH COMES ALONG WITH POSITIVE CHANGE.

 FRIDAY, MAY 14TH, 2021. I CRIED DURING THERAPY—CLASSIC.

HOW ARE YOU?

DO YOU FEEL TIRED?

IS TIME GOING TOO FAST FOR YOU?

MAYBE YOU CAN TAKE A NAP

AFTER A GOOD CRY.

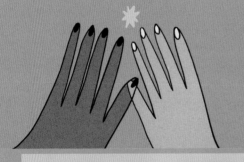

LET IT ALL OUT

RELEASING EMOTIONAL TENSION WITH TEARS IS LIKE DISINFECTING A SCRATCH. AT FIRST, CLEANING A FRESH WOUND WITH WATER MIGHT REALLY HURT. BUT THE SOONER YOU WASH IT OUT, THE FASTER IT HEALS.

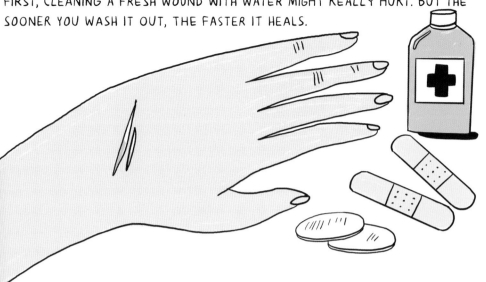

IN 2015, I STARTED DOING TRANSCENDENTAL MEDITATION. MY INTRODUCTION TO TM, A TECHNIQUE THAT INVOLVES THE USE OF A SILENTLY REPEATED PHRASE CALLED A MANTRA, WAS THROUGH A CERTIFIED INSTRUCTOR. I SPENT FIVE DAYS AT HER HOUSE LEARNING HOW TO PRACTICE, AND EVERY TIME WE MEDITATED, I CRIED WHAT FELT LIKE SURREAL TEARS. MY INSTRUCTOR SAID I WAS RELEASING OLD TENSIONS FROM THE PAST, WHICH COULD EVEN BE GENERATIONAL TENSIONS. TURNS OUT THAT CRYING WHILE MEDITATING CAN BE VERY COMMON.

DURING THE MIDDLE AGES, TEARS WERE CONSIDERED TO BE A POWERFUL AND EFFICACIOUS FLUID: THEY COULD CURE INFECTIONS AND RELEASE SOULS FROM PURGATORY; THEY CERTIFIED HOLINESS AND IDENTIFIED DISHONESTY; THEY WERE SHED IN LOVING DEVOTION AND SPIRITUAL CONNECTION TO HOLY FIGURES; AND THEY WERE ASSOCIATED WITH A VISIONARY EXPERIENCE AND CLEANED OUT AGENTS THAT OBSCURED VISION.

THE BOOK OF HOLY MEDICINES—WRITTEN BY HENRY OF GROSMONT IN 1354—OFFERED A RECIPE FOR A MAGICAL AND MIRACULOUS BALM, A CONCENTRATE THAT MIXED CHRIST'S BLOOD AND MARY'S TEARS INTO A KIND OF SPIRITUAL ROSEWATER. THIS DIVINE CLEANSER ALLEGEDLY HEALED THE BODY, THE MIND, AND THE SOUL.

 THURSDAY, MARCH 9TH, 2023. I SAW MY HEART FOR THE FIRST TIME. THE ULTRASOUND TECHNICIAN SAID, "IT'S BEAUTIFUL," AND I CRIED.

IN DIFFERENT FOLKLORE TRADITIONS, MERMAID TEARS TURN INTO BEAUTIFUL GLOSSY PEARLS.

A SEA OF SHINY TEARS

 MONDAY, FEBRUARY 8TH, 2021. I SHED NOSTALGIC TEARS WHILE JOURNALING OF THE PAST.

TEARS OF LOVE

A WIDESPREAD THEORY IN THE 1600S STATED THAT POWERFUL EMOTIONS LIKE LOVE WARMED UP THE HEART. THE PUMPING ORGAN GENERATED WATER VAPOR IN ORDER TO COOL ITSELF DOWN.

THE HEART VAPOR RISES TO THE HEAD,

CONDENSES NEAR THE EYES,

AND ESCAPES AS TEARS.

SUNDAY, MAY 22ND, 2022. I CRIED WITH PURE LOVE IN THE GROCERY STORE LINE.

TEAR CATCHERS

LACHRYMATORIES, OR TEAR BOTTLES, HAVE A HISTORY THAT DATES BACK TO 400 BCE. THESE POCKET-SIZE RECEPTACLES ARE EMBELLISHED GLASS CONTAINERS THAT HOLD SHARED TEARS OF LOVE, JOY, CONDOLENCE, AND REMEMBRANCE.

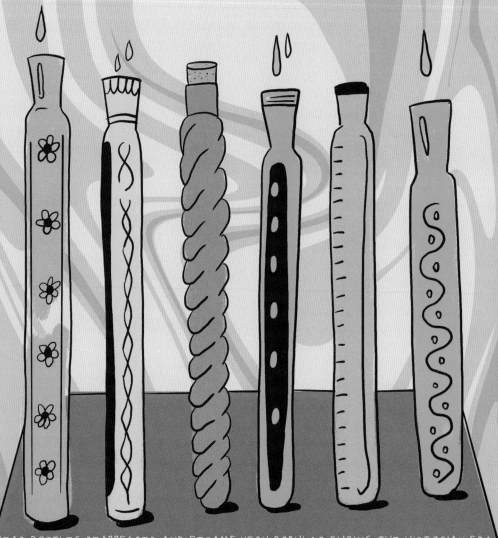

TEAR BOTTLES REAPPEARED AND BECAME VERY POPULAR DURING THE VICTORIAN ERA. PEOPLE MOURNING THE LOSS OF A LOVED ONE WOULD COLLECT THEIR TEARS IN A SMALL DECORATED BOTTLE. INSIDE THIS GLASS HOLDER THE TEARS WOULD EVAPORATE. WHEN THE TEARS WERE FINALLY GONE, THE MOURNING PERIOD WOULD END.

WEEPING HAS BEEN A SIGNIFICANT ASPECT OF ADMIRATION IN VARIOUS CULTURES FOR CENTURIES. THROUGHOUT THOUSANDS OF YEARS, MATURE MEN AND WOMEN EVEN INTENTIONALLY CRIED IN PUBLIC, HOPING TO IMPRESS OTHERS.

MOST INDIVIDUALS CLAIM FEELING UNCOMFORTABLE AROUND OTHER PEOPLE'S TEARS, ALTHOUGH THEY ACKNOWLEDGE THAT SOMETHING STRONGLY HUMBLING IS GOING ON. SO IF TEARS ARE A RELEASE OF PSYCHOLOGICAL TOXINS AND CAN ALSO EXPRESS PURE LOVE, WHY ARE WE SO AFRAID OF THEM?

The Crying Times

BREAKING NEWS:
HUMANS HAVE BEEN CRYING FOR
THOUSANDS OF YEARS

MOURNING ISIS,
332—30 BCE EGYPT

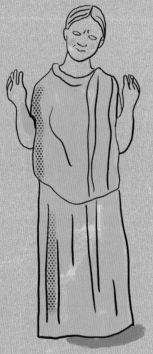

STATUE OF A MOURNING WOMAN,
300—275 BCE GREECE

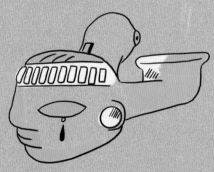

CRYING AZTEC CHILD,
WHISTLING JUG, 1000—1400

THE MAGDALEN WEEPING,
CIRCA 1525

VICTORIAN WOMAN
CRYING

THE WEEPING FRENCHMAN,
1940

CRYING GUY,
2020

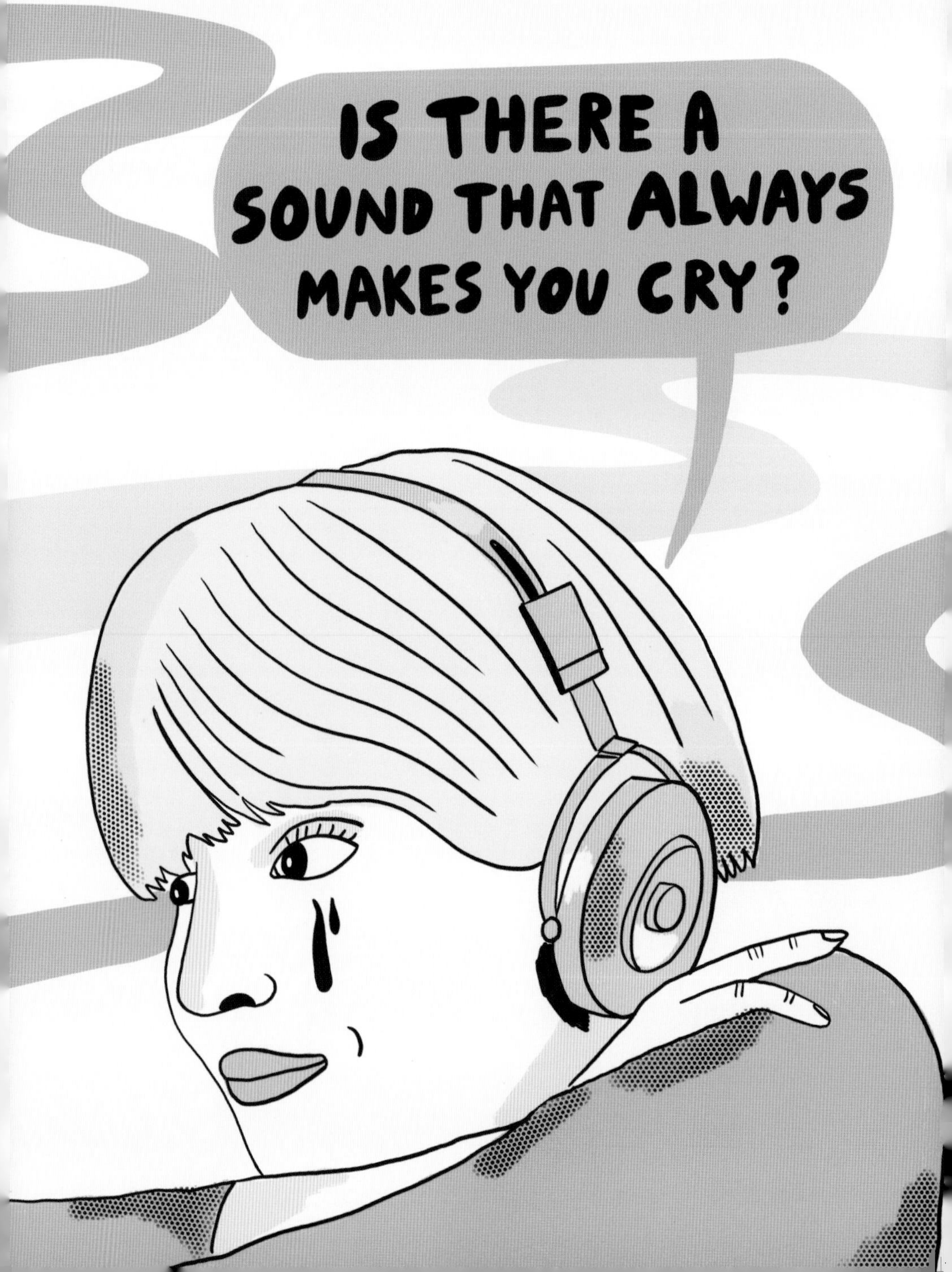
IS THERE A SOUND THAT ALWAYS MAKES YOU CRY?

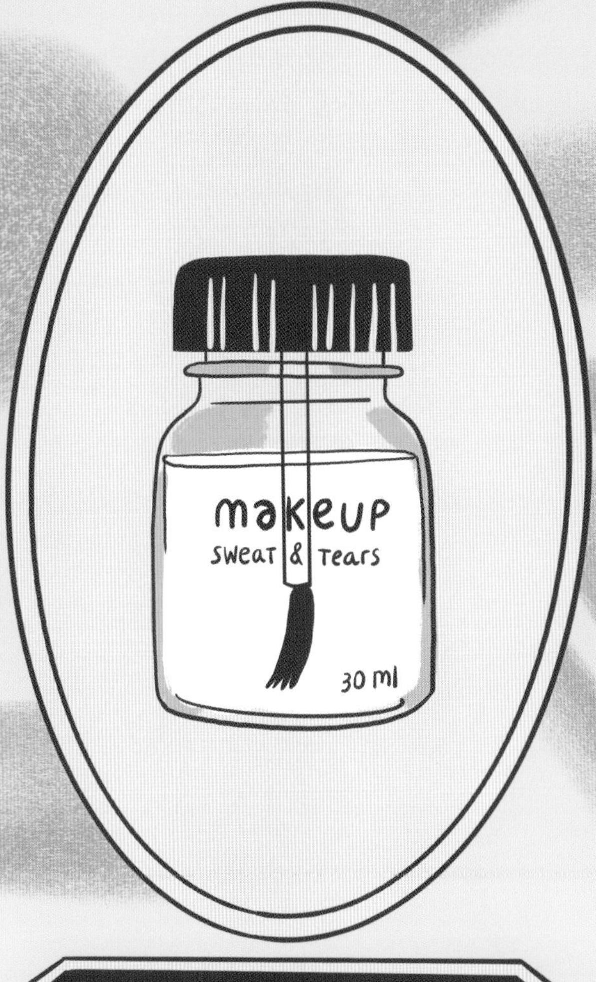
makeup
sweat & tears
30 ml

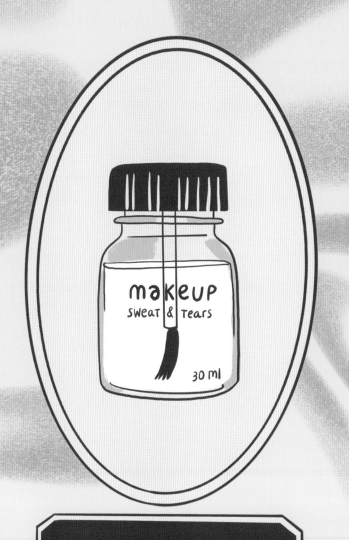

CROCODILE TEARS

GROWING UP IN THE SOUTHERN HEMISPHERE, WE CELEBRATED CHRISTMAS DURING SUMMER. ONE CHRISTMAS EVE, WHEN I WAS ELEVEN YEARS OLD, MY FATHER WAS PREPARING TO COOK OUR TRADITIONAL FESTIVE BARBECUE. I WANTED TO GO FOR A BIKE RIDE WITH MY NEIGHBOR. MY DAD DIDN'T LET ME GO OUT AND ASKED ME TO SHOWER AND GET READY FOR THE FAMILY DINNER. FRUSTRATED, I LOCKED MYSELF IN MY ROOM AND SPENT THE REST OF THE NIGHT CRYING.

I CRIED FAKE TEARS. I SOBBED AS LOUD AS I COULD. I WANTED TO GET HIS ATTENTION SO HE WOULD KNOW MY SUFFERING WAS HIS FAULT. I FELL ASLEEP EXHAUSTED FROM ALL THE CRYING WITHOUT EATING DINNER. THE NEXT MORNING, MY DAD WOKE ME UP WITH A KISS AND A PLATE OF LEFTOVERS.

WE KNOW THAT CROCODILE TEARS ARE A FORM OF SUPERFICIAL SADNESS,
FALSE TEARS THAT ARE AN INSINCERE DISPLAY OF EMOTION. THE EXPRESSION
DERIVES FROM AN ANCIENT IDEA THAT CROCODILES SHED TEARS WHILE
CONSUMING THEIR PREY, AND THE PHRASE IS PART OF MANY MODERN
LANGUAGES AND CULTURES.

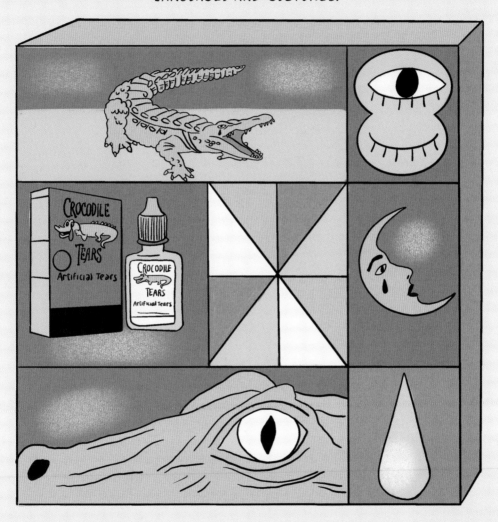

ALTHOUGH CROCODILES DO HAVE TEAR DUCTS, THEY WEEP TO LUBRICATE
THEIR EYES, USUALLY AFTER BEING OUT OF WATER FOR LONG
ENOUGH THAT THEIR EYES HAVE DRIED OUT.

TEARS AND IDEAS

SOME EIGHTEENTH-CENTURY WRITERS EXPLORED THE RELATIONSHIP BETWEEN CRYING AND SINCERITY. IN ONE OF HIS PHILOSOPHICAL WORKS, JEAN-JACQUES ROUSSEAU EXPLAINS HOW EMOTIONS IN CULTURE ARE IMITATIONS OF THE PRIMITIVE EMOTIONS PEOPLE FEEL IN THEIR MOST NATURAL, UNADULTERATED, AND WHOLEHEARTED STATE.

MORE RECENTLY, ROLAND BARTHES WROTE, "BY WEEPING, I WANT TO IMPRESS SOMEONE, TO BRING PRESSURE TO BEAR UPON SOMEONE...I MAKE MYSELF CRY IN ORDER TO PROVE TO MYSELF THAT MY GRIEF IS NOT AN ILLUSION; TEARS ARE SIGNS, NOT EXPRESSIONS. BY MY TEARS, I TELL A STORY, I PRODUCE A MYTH OF GRIEF, AND HENCEFORTH I ADJUST MYSELF TO IT: I CAN LIVE WITH IT, BECAUSE, BY WEEPING, I GIVE MYSELF AN EMPHATIC INTERLOCUTOR WHO RECEIVES THE 'TRUEST' OF MESSAGES, THAT OF MY BODY, NOT THAT OF MY SPEECH: 'WORDS, WHAT ARE THEY? ONE TEAR WILL SAY MORE THAN ALL OF THEM.'"

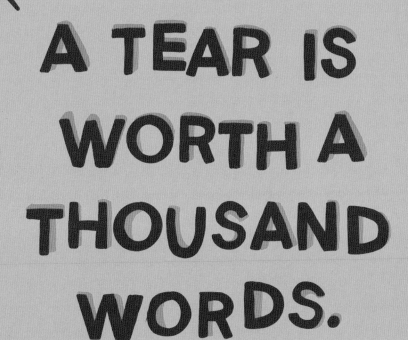

A TEAR IS WORTH A THOUSAND WORDS.

SHAKESPEARE OFTEN USED THE IDEA OF FAKE TEARS IN HIS WORK. THE WORDS "WEEP" OR "TEARS" APPEAR MORE THAN SIX HUNDRED TIMES IN HIS PLAYS, ALMOST EVERY TIME ALLUDING TO SOMEONE CRYING FALSE TEARS TO GET SOMEONE ELSE'S ATTENTION. IN *OTHELLO*, FOR INSTANCE, THERE ARE A FEW PASSAGES IN WHICH THE MAIN CHARACTER CONVINCES HIMSELF THAT HIS WIFE IS CHEATING ON HIM, AND THAT SHE'S FAKING HER CRYING.

IF THAT THE EARTH COULD TEEM WITH WOMAN'S TEARS, EACH DROP SHE FALLS WOULD PROVE A CROCODILE.

BEING MOVED BY WATCHING SOMEONE ELSE CRY FICTIONAL TEARS CAN MAKE US PAY ATTENTION TO OUR OWN CONFLICTS, ASPIRATIONS, AND DESIRES.

 WEDNESDAY, SEPTEMBER 22ND, 2021. I CRIED WATCHING DAVID BYRNE'S *AMERICAN UTOPIA* ON BROADWAY.

PAID FOR THEIR TEARS

PROFESSIONAL MOURNERS ARE PEOPLE HIRED TO CRY AT FUNERALS. THE PRACTICE OF PROFESSIONAL MOURNING HARKENS BACK TO ANCIENT TIMES IN EGYPT, CHINA, AND THE MIDDLE EAST.

IN EASTERN CULTURES, THE HIRED MOURNER PERFORMS A SPECIFIC CATHARTIC ROLE FOR THE FAMILY AND FRIENDS.

IN SOME REMOTE VILLAGES OF GREECE AND ITALY, ELDERLY WOMEN ARE STILL HIRED AS "MOIROLOGISTS" NOT JUST TO GRIEVE PEOPLE THEY DON'T KNOW BUT ALSO TO SING AND CRY AS THEY LEAD A FAMILY THROUGH THE FINAL MOMENTS WITH THEIR LOVED ONE. THE SONGS THEY PERFORM RETELL AND IMPROVISE THE STORY OF THE DEAD PERSON's LIFE.

IN ENGLAND, YOU CAN STILL HIRE A PROFESSIONAL MOURNER THROUGH COMPANIES LIKE RENT-A-MOURNER THAT PAY ACTORS TO PLAY A DISTANT COUSIN OR UNCLE, HELPING FAMILIES INCREASE THE NUMBER OF FUNERAL GUESTS.

THE FULL MOURNER PACKAGE INCLUDES BLENDING WITH THE CROWD AND HELPING PEOPLE TALK AND GRIEVE. THE MOURNER'S JOB IS TO ENCOURAGE PEOPLE TO SHARE STORIES, CRY, AND GET CLOSURE.

RENT-A-MOURNER

WE'LL CRY FOR YOU

RENT-A-MOURNER

RENT-A-MOURNER

WE'LL CRY FOR YOU

RENT-A-MOURNER

WE'LL CRY FOR YOU

RENT-A-MOURNER

WE'LL CRY FOR YOU

IN 2016, ARTIST TARYN SIMON TOOK THIRTY PROFESSIONAL MOURNERS TO MANHATTAN FROM BURKINA FASO, CAMBODIA, RUSSIA, VENEZUELA, AND OTHER PARTS OF THE GLOBE TO PERFORM BEFORE HER MULTIDISCIPLINARY ARTWORK *AN OCCUPATION OF LOSS*. SIMON'S INSTALLATION CONSIDERED THE ANATOMY OF GRIEF AND THE INTRICATE SYSTEMS WE USE TO MANAGE CONTINGENCIES OF FATE AND THE UNCERTAINTY OF THE UNIVERSE.

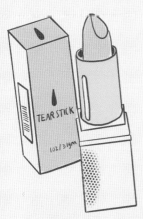

NATURAL TEARS ON CUE: A MENTHOL-INFUSED FORMULA RELEASES VAPORS UPON CONTACT WITH THE WARMTH OF YOUR SKIN, CAUSING NATURAL TEARS TO FORM. PERFECT FOR ACTORS AND ACTRESSES.

1 CLEAN SKIN JUST BELOW EYE WITH A FACIAL CLEANSER OR MAKEUP REMOVER.

2 APPLY TEAR STICK TO SKIN ABOUT 0.5 IN. / 15MM UNDER THE EYE.

3 THE TEMPERATURE OF THE SKIN WILL WARM THE WAX, RELEASING MENTHOL VAPORS, CAUSING REAL, NATURAL TEARS TO FORM.

4 APPLY MULTIPLE LAYERS FOR A STRONGER EFFECT. REMOVE WITH SOAP AND WATER, FACIAL CLEANSER, OR MAKEUP REMOVER.*

 WEDNESDAY, APRIL 1ST, 2020. I CRIED CUTTING SOME ONIONS AND TOOK THE OPPORTUNITY TO CRY ABOUT OTHER THINGS.

*Information on tear-inducing cosmetic products appearing in this book is not intended to be advice or a recommendation concerning any cosmetic product.

IF YOU FIND IT IMPOSSIBLE TO START CRYING, JULIO CORTÁZAR'S "INSTRUCTIONS ON HOW TO CRY" RECOMMENDS PICTURING A DUCK COVERED WITH ANTS, OR BODIES OF WATER INTO WHICH NO ONE EVER SAILS.

MY OWN CRYING INSTRUCTIONS:

REWATCH *TITANIC* WHILE EATING VERY SPICY FOOD.

GRAB A BIKE AND RIDE DOWN A HILL AT MAXIMUM SPEED.

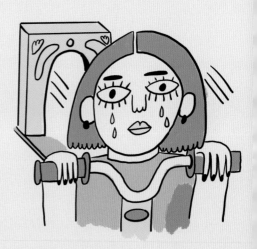

GO TO THE NEAREST TRAIN STATION AND WAIT FOR THE TRAIN AT 2 A.M. ON A COLD WINTER NIGHT.

LEAVE YOUR PHONE AT HOME AND WAIT IN LINE AT THE POST OFFICE THE WEEK BEFORE CHRISTMAS.

GO TO THE PARK AND HOLD A
CHILD'S POSE FOR TWO HOURS.

KEEP YOUR EYES WIDE OPEN
AS LONG AS YOU CAN.

IN EMOTIONAL SCENES, FILMMAKERS MAY REQUIRE ACTORS TO SHED REAL TEARS TO CONVEY INTENSE AND GENUINE EMOTIONS. ONE TECHNIQUE ACTORS USE IS AFFECTIVE MEMORY, WHEREBY THEY EXPERIENCE THE SAME EMOTIONS AS THEIR CHARACTERS BY TAPPING INTO THEIR OWN MEMORIES OR THROUGH A PROFOUND SENSE OF EMPATHY. THIS EMOTION DOESN'T NECESSARILY HAVE TO BE TRIGGERED BY THE ROLE ITSELF; SOMETHING UNRELATED THAT THE ACTOR SAW OR READ ABOUT MIGHT EVOKE THE CHARACTER'S EMOTION EVEN BETTER THAN THE SCRIPT.

EMOTIONAL MEMORY

THE ACTOR PROBABLY CONJURES THESE "CROCODILE TEARS" BY THINKING OF SOMETHING SAD, LIKE THE DEATH OF A LOVED ONE, OR A CHILDHOOD UPSET. THIS METHOD WAS FIRST INTRODUCED BY KONSTANTIN STANISLAVSKI.

TOWARD THE END OF HIS LIFE AND HIS CAREER, STANISLAVSKI BEGAN TO QUESTION THE SAFETY OF AFFECTIVE MEMORY. THE METHOD IS EXHAUSTING AND CAN HAVE NEGATIVE SIDE EFFECTS IF THE ACTOR DRAWS ON BAD MEMORIES WITHOUT A THERAPIST OR COUNSELOR TO HELP. THE STANISLAVSKI METHOD ASKS THAT YOU DON'T "ASSAULT THE SUBCONSCIOUS." HE PREFERRED USING PAST MEMORIES TO PRESENT SITUATIONS, AS THEY'RE MORE EASILY CONTROLLED.

STANISLAVSKI IMPLORED ACTORS TO TRY TO REMEMBER THE GOOD TIMES TOO.

SENSE MEMORY, TAUGHT BY LEE STRASBERG, IS A VARIANT OF AFFECTIVE MEMORY. THIS TAKE ON THE METHOD ACTING SYSTEM ASKS THAT THE ACTOR TAKE TIME OUT TO RECALL EVERY DETAIL OF THEIR MEMORY. THEY MUST REMEMBER NOT JUST THE EMOTION, BUT WHAT THEY HEARD, TASTED, TOUCHED, SMELLED, AND SAW WHILE FEELING IT.

 WEDNESDAY, DECEMBER 16TH, 2020. I CRIED WHILE WATCHING AN OLD VIDEO OF ME CRYING.

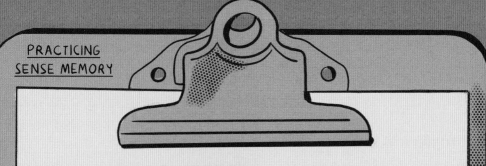

CLOSE YOUR EYES AND...

SEE:

* YOUR PARENTS' FACES, IN AS MUCH DETAIL AS POSSIBLE.

* THE OUTFIT YOU WORE TO YOUR FIRST DANCE PARTY.

* A STARRY SUMMER SKY FROM YOUR CHILDHOOD.

HEAR:

* RAIN AGAINST THE WINDOW.

* WAVES THAT COME AND GO.

* THE VOICE OF YOUR BEST FRIEND.

SMELL:

* SMOKE FROM A BONFIRE.

* FRESHLY BAKED BREAD.

TASTE:

* ICE CREAM.

* BUTTERY TOAST.

FEEL:

* A HOT MUG OF TEA IN YOUR HANDS.

* A FEATHER TICKLING YOUR CHEEKS.

DID YOU CRY ON THE INSIDE?

MY EARLIEST RECOLLECTION OF CRYING DURING A FILM IS FROM 1994. I WAS
EIGHT YEARS OLD, AND I WAS WATCHING THE MOVIE *MY GIRL* ON TV.
IN THIS COMING-OF-AGE DRAMA, THE PROTAGONIST, A GIRL NAMED VADA,
BEFRIENDS THOMAS, AN UNPOPULAR BOY WHO IS ALLERGIC TO EVERYTHING.
THEY SPEND THE WHOLE SUMMER TOGETHER, AND THEY WONDER WHAT A FIRST
KISS FEELS LIKE UNDER A WILLOW TREE. VADA LOSES HER MOOD RING IN THE
WOODS. A FEW DAYS LATER THOMAS RETURNS TO THE WILLOW TREE TO FIND THE
RING, AND THERE HE KNOCKS DOWN A BEEHIVE AND IS KILLED BY THOUSANDS OF BEES.

VADA GRIEVES FOR HER FRIEND AS WELL AS HER CHILDHOOD. BY THE END OF THE
MOVIE, I WAS SO SHATTERED FOR HER THAT I CRIED ALL NIGHT. FOR THE FIRST
TIME, I FELT LIKE THE TEARS WERE GLUING MY HEART TOGETHER.

 MONDAY, FEBRUARY 17TH, 2020. THIS WEEK I CRIED WATCHING *MY GIRL*,
WHICH MADE ME CRY JUST AS MUCH AS THE FIRST TIME I SAW IT.

KINTSUGI IS THE JAPANESE ART OF REPAIRING BROKEN POTTERY BY FIXING THE CRACKS AND BROKEN AREAS WITH LACQUER DUSTED OR MIXED WITH POWDERED GOLD, SILVER, OR PLATINUM. THE CRACKS ARE HIGHLIGHTED RATHER THAN HIDDEN.

SOMETIMES CRYING MENDS THE HEART AND TEARS ACT AS A PRECIOUS METAL.

THE SUMMER THE MOVIE *TITANIC* OPENED IN THEATERS, I WAS TWELVE YEARS OLD, AND I HAD A BIG CRUSH ON LEONARDO DICAPRIO. I WENT TO SEE IT AT THE MOVIE THEATER MORE THAN SEVEN TIMES. EVERY TIME—AT THE CLIMAX OF THE FILM—A BIG LUMP FORMED IN MY THROAT AND THE TEAR FLOODGATES OPENED WIDE. MY EYES BECAME LIKE TWO WATER FOUNTAINS. I COULDN'T STOP CRYING ABOUT JACK'S DEATH AND THE FACT THAT I MIGHT NEVER GET TO MEET LEO DICAPRIO IN PERSON.

LEO DICAPRIO KATE WINSLET
TITANIC

YEARS LATER, I SAW LEONARDO DICAPRIO AT THE ELECTRIC ROOM IN NEW YORK CITY, THE NIGHT OF MY TWENTY-SEVENTH BIRTHDAY. I DIDN'T CRY.

A STUDY HAS SHOWN THAT THE ABILITY TO CRY DURING MOVIES ACTUALLY REQUIRES SOME SERIOUSLY FORMIDABLE EMOTIONAL STRENGTH. THIS EXPERIENCE OF GREAT EMPATHY, IN WHICH WE IMMERSE OURSELVES IN SOMEONE ELSE'S FEELINGS, EVEN IF THEY ARE FICTIONAL, DEMONSTRATES THE DEPTH OF OUR EMOTIONAL CAPACITY.

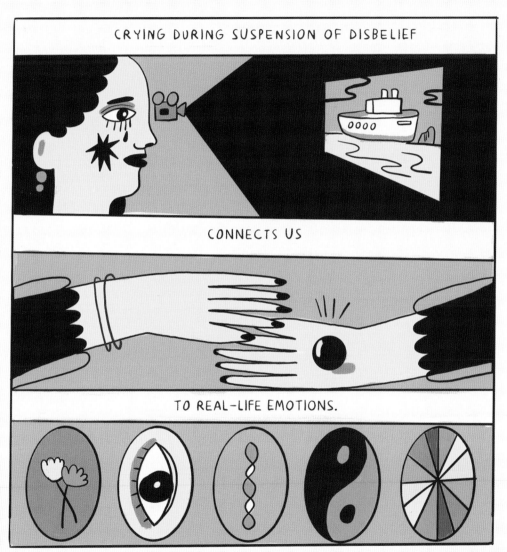

CONSUMING SAD STORIES ENABLES US TO EXPERIENCE SADNESS WITHOUT ANXIETY, MAKES US FEEL MORE GRATEFUL FOR OUR CLOSE RELATIONSHIPS, AND CAUSES US TO THINK ABOUT WHAT'S VALUABLE AND MEANINGFUL IN OUR OWN LIVES.

YOU'VE GOT MAIL: THE OWNER OF A STRUGGLING BOUTIQUE BOOKSHOP, KATHLEEN KELLY (MEG RYAN), HATES JOE FOX (TOM HANKS), THE OWNER OF A CORPORATE CHAIN STORE THAT JUST MOVED IN ACROSS THE STREET. WHEN THEY MEET ANONYMOUSLY ONLINE, HOWEVER, THEY BEGIN AN INTENSE INTERNET ROMANCE, WITHOUT KNOWING OF EACH OTHER'S TRUE IDENTITY. EVENTUALLY THEY LEARN THEY ARE BUSINESS RIVALS.

* CRYINGOMETER 82%

* THIS MOVIE WILL HAVE YOU SOBBING AS YOU IDENTIFY THE MECHANISMS THAT CONTRIBUTE TO THE CONSTRUCTION OF ROMANTIC LOVE.

FANTASIA: A 1940s ANIMATED MUSICAL FILM SEQUENCE PRODUCED AND RELEASED BY WALT DISNEY PRODUCTIONS. IT CONSISTS OF EIGHT ANIMATED SEGMENTS SET TO PIECES OF CLASSICAL MUSIC, CONDUCTED BY LEOPOLD STOKOWSKI.

* CRYINGOMETER 88%

* YOUR LIPS WILL BE QUIVERING WITH DROPS OF NOSTALGIC AND VERY CLASSICAL TEARS.

STEPMOM: THIS '90s HEARTBREAKER FOLLOWS THE STORY OF ISABEL (JULIA ROBERTS), WHO TRIES TO FORM A BOND WITH HER NEW FIANCÉ'S TWO KIDS WHILE COMPETING WITH THEIR MOTHER, JACKIE HARRISON (SUSAN SARANDON), WHO IS BATTLING CANCER. THROUGH THE JOURNEY OF HEARTACHE, LOVE, AND LOSS, BOTH WOMEN MUST LEARN TO COME TOGETHER TO SUPPORT THE CHILDREN AND EACH OTHER.

* CRYINGOMETER 100%

* YOU WILL NEED SEVERAL BOXES OF TISSUES AND A PHONE CALL TO SOMEONE YOU LOVE AFTERWARD.

SPIRITED AWAY: THIS MOVIE FOLLOWS THE TRANSFORMATION OF THE MAIN CHARACTER, CHIHIRO, INTO A STRONGER, MORE MATURE PERSON AS SHE IS FORCED TO SURVIVE IN A WORLD COMPLETELY ALIEN TO HER. THE JOURNEY IS FANTASTICAL AND DAUNTING AS CHIHIRO COMES UP AGAINST INTENSELY FRIGHTENING FORCES.

* CRYINGOMETER 86%

* A TEARFUL ANIMATED REMINDER OF HOW CONFUSING IT IS TO GROW UP.

DANCER IN THE DARK: A CZECH IMMIGRANT NAMED SELMA IS A SINGLE MOTHER WORKING IN A FACTORY IN RURAL AMERICA. HER ONLY ESCAPE IS HER PASSION FOR MUSIC, SPECIFICALLY SONGS IN CLASSIC HOLLYWOOD MUSICALS. SELMA HAS A SAD SECRET: SHE IS LOSING HER EYESIGHT, AND HER SON, GENE, STANDS TO SUFFER THE SAME FATE IF SHE CAN'T PUT AWAY ENOUGH MONEY TO PAY FOR HIS OPERATION.

* CRYINGOMETER 97%

* JUST WHEN YOU THINK YOU'RE DONE CRYING, IT'LL MAKE YOU CRY EVEN MORE.

THE BICYCLE THIEF: THIS FILM PORTRAYS A POOR FAMILY STRUGGLING TO SURVIVE. THE FATHER FINALLY GETS A JOB, ONLY TO HAVE HIS BICYCLE STOLEN BY THIEVES. THE FATHER AND HIS SON WORK TOGETHER TO TRY TO FIND THE BIKE.

* CRYINGOMETER 95%

* THIS MOVIE ABOUT POST-WAR EVERYDAY REALITY WILL MAKE YOU CRY NEO-REALISTIC TEARS.

HAROLD AND MAUDE: A DISILLUSIONED TWENTY-YEAR-OLD OBSESSED WITH SUICIDE AND A LOVABLE EIGHTY-YEAR-OLD ECCENTRIC MEET AT A FUNERAL AND DEVELOP A TABOO ROMANTIC RELATIONSHIP, IN WHICH THEY EXPLORE THE MEANING OF LIFE.

* CRYINGOMETER 90%

* YOU WILL CRY BIZARRE AND PHILOSOPHICAL TEARS.

PETITE MAMAN: NELLY, AN EIGHT-YEAR-OLD GIRL, HAS JUST LOST HER BELOVED GRANDMOTHER AND IS HELPING HER PARENTS CLEAN OUT HER MOTHER'S CHILDHOOD HOME. ONE DAY, HER MUM ABRUPTLY LEAVES, AND NELLY MEETS A GIRL HER AGE AS SHE'S BUILDING A TREE HOUSE IN THE WOODS.

* CRYINGOMETER 92%

* YOU WILL SUDDENLY CRY IN FRENCH.

THE SOUND OF TEARS

CRYING TO MUSIC IS EVEN MORE MYSTERIOUS THAN CRYING IN MOVIES. A PHYSIOLOGICAL EXPERIMENT FOUND THAT SONGS THAT BROUGHT OUT BOTH CHILLS AND TEARS RESULTED IN A MORE INTENSE BREATHING PATTERN AND A FEELING OF PLEASURE. DURING THE STUDY, A SONG THAT BROUGHT OUT CHILLS WAS PERCEIVED AS BEING BOTH HAPPY AND SAD, WHEREAS A SONG THAT PROVOKED TEARS WAS PERCEIVED AS SAD. A TEAR-INDUCING MELODY WAS PERCEIVED AS CALMER AND SOFTER THAN A CHILL-INDUCING SONG.

 MONDAY, DECEMBER 28TH, 2020. I CRIED LISTENING TO BOLEROS BY ARMANDO MANZANERO.

CLASSICAL MUSIC OFTEN PRODUCES BOTH CHILLS AND TEARS—OR BRAIN "TINGLES."
HEARING THIS KIND OF MUSIC MAY GENERATE A QUICK PHYSIOLOGICAL RESPONSE
THAT ACTIVATES AND LIGHTS UP THE PARASYMPATHETIC NERVOUS SYSTEM
AS WELL AS THE REWARD-RELATED REGIONS OF THE BRAIN.

STUDIES HAVE SHOWN THAT AROUND 25 PERCENT OF THE
POPULATION EXPERIENCES THIS EMOTIONAL REACTION. CLASSICAL
MUSIC IN PARTICULAR SETS IN MOTION A MYSTERIOUS,
UNEXPECTED, AND POWERFUL EMOTIONAL RESPONSE, WHICH CAN
RESULT IN MELANCHOLIC OR JOYFUL TEARS.

DURING DIFFICULT TIMES, I HAVE SPENT HOURS LISTENING TO JONI MITCHELL ON REPEAT. IN THE SONG "BLUE," SHE SINGS, "SONGS ARE LIKE TATTOOS"—THE TEARS I SHED EVERY TIME I LISTEN TO THESE WORDS FEEL LIKE NEEDLES PINCHING MY CHEEKS. THE SONG IS LIKE AN ARROW THAT GOES DIRECTLY INTO MY HEART.

DAVID BOWIE RECORDED THE SONG "FIVE YEARS" WHILE CRYING. KEN SCOTT, BOWIE'S CO-PRODUCER, MENTIONED THAT THE MUSICIAN SHED TEARS AS HE FINISHED HIS PERFORMANCE OF THE FIRST TRACK FOR THE ALBUM *THE RISE AND FALL OF ZIGGY STARDUST AND THE SPIDERS FROM MARS*. THE EMOTION OF THE SONG WAS SO IMMENSE THAT BY THE END OF THE TAKE HE WAS BAWLING HIS EYES OUT; THERE WERE SUBSTANTIAL TEARS ROLLING DOWN HIS FACE AS HE PERFECTLY HIT EVERY NOTE.

CRYING PLAYLIST:

* "CRYING" BY ROY ORBISON

* "HOMESICKNESS, Pt. 2" BY EMAHOY TSEGUÉ-MARYAM GUÈBROU

* "I FOUND A REASON" BY THE VELVET UNDERGROUND

* "ALFONSINA Y EL MAR" BY MERCEDES SOSA, ARIEL RAMIREZ, AND HECTOR ZEOLI

* "MOTHER NATURE'S SON" BY THE BEATLES

* "BALTIMORE" BY NINA SIMONE

* "LISTEN BEFORE I GO" BY BILLIE EILISH

* "ALL I COULD DO WAS CRY" BY ETTA JAMES

* "STRANGE FRUIT" BY BILLIE HOLIDAY

* "WHAT THE WORLD NEEDS NOW IS LOVE" BY DIONNE WARWICK

* "SOMEONE GREAT" BY LCD SOUNDSYSTEM

* "I THINK OF ANGELS" BY CAT POWER

CRYING MIX TAPE

LITERARY TEARS

CRYING WHILE READING IS A DELICATE ACTIVITY; YOU CAN REALLY STAIN AND BEND A BOOK'S PAGES. A BOOK THAT MAKES YOU CRY IS A MANIFESTATION OF ALL THE POSSIBLE LIVES THAT YOU CAN LIVE. WE CAN BECOME THOSE CHARACTERS AND SUFFER AND LOVE LIKE THEM, SEE THE WORLD THROUGH THEIR EYES.

IT IS A CELESTIAL SENSATION

WHEN A BOOK SPEAKS DIRECTLY TO MY SOUL,

AND I SHED TEARS OF EMOTION.

THERE IS ONE BOOK I WOULD DEFINITELY TAKE TO A DESERT ISLAND, AND IT'S *LITTLE WOMEN* BY LOUISA MAY ALCOTT. I READ AND REREAD THIS NOVEL BECAUSE IT MAKES ME FEEL THINGS. THE STORY FOLLOWS THE LIVES OF THE FOUR MARCH SISTERS—MEG, JO, BETH, AND AMY—AND DETAILS THEIR PASSAGE FROM CHILDHOOD TO WOMANHOOD. IT HAS MADE ME CRY A THOUSAND TIMES. I FEEL CONNECTED TO THE FOUR SISTERS IN VERY DIFFERENT WAYS, THROUGH FAMILIAR INTIMACY, WORK LIFE, AND TRUE LOVE. ALL OF THEIR DISTINCT PERSONALITY TRAITS FELT LIKE NECESSARY ELEMENTS IN THE DISCOVERY OF MY OWN PERSONAL IDENTITY.

INCONSOLABLE TEARS ARRIVE IN MY EYES EVERY TIME BETH MARCH DIES. MY THROAT CLOSES UP AND BIG HEAVY TEARS START TO PRECIPITATE LIKE A NOSTALGIC SNOWSTORM FROM THE SOUL.

IN THE EIGHTEENTH CENTURY, THE NOVEL EMERGED AS A POPULAR FORM OF STORYTELLING, AND CRYING WHILE READING WAS A WAY FOR THE READER TO SIGNAL THEIR SENSITIVITY AND CONNECTION WITH THE STORY. SENTIMENTAL NOVELS, OVERFLOWING WITH TENDER AND UPSETTING SCENES, GAVE READERS AN OPPORTUNITY TO EXPLORE THEIR FINER FEELINGS.

THESE LITERARY TEARS PROVED THE READER FELT EMPATHY TOWARD THE SUFFERING OF OTHERS.

THE WRITER JEAN-JACQUES ROUSSEAU USED TO RECEIVE FAN MAIL THAT TALKED ABOUT HOW READERS WERE CRYING OVER SOME OF HIS FAMOUS SENTIMENTAL NOVELS, LIKE *JULIE; OR, THE NEW HELOISE.*

SOME OF THESE LETTERS READ:

"ONE MUST WRITE TO YOU THAT ONE IS CHOKING WITH EMOTION AND WEEPING."

"NEVER HAVE I WEPT SUCH DELICIOUS TEARS."

"I VERILY BELIEVE I HAVE SHED A PINT OF TEARS."

DURING THE NINETEENTH CENTURY, THE LITERARY SIGNIFICANCE OF TEARS EXPANDED IN TWO DIRECTIONS. SOME AUTHORS WANTED TO EVOKE MORE "PROFOUND" EMOTIONAL RESPONSES IN READERS. VICTORIAN SENTIMENTALISTS, LIKE DICKENS, WROTE TRAGIC SCENES, OFTEN REVOLVING AROUND THE DEATH OF SMALL CHILDREN, WITH THE HOPES OF INSPIRING SOME KIND OF SOCIAL CHANGE. OTHER WRITERS BECAME ADDICTED TO THE IDEA OF ENJOYING EMOTION AND POPULARIZED THE "SENSATION" NOVEL.

THESE AUTHORS WERE FAMOUS FOR CREATING PHYSICAL REACTIONS IN THEIR READERS—GOOSE BUMPS, COLD CHILLS, BLUSHING CHEEKS, AND DRAMATIC TEARS. THESE TEARS DIDN'T HAVE A REAL PURPOSE; THE OBJECTIVE WAS JUST TO GENERATE AN INTENSE SENSATION. WHILE THESE NOVELS BECAME BEST SELLERS AMONG READERS, CRITICS FOUND SENSATION NOVELS TACKY.

LITERARY MODERNISM, WHICH EMERGED IN THE LATE NINETEENTH AND EARLY
TWENTIETH CENTURIES, WANTED TO BREAK WITH TRADITIONAL WRITING
CONVENTIONS AND EXPERIMENT WITH NEW FORMS OF WRITTEN EXPRESSION.
MODERNIST LITERATURE ENGAGED WITH THE CRUELTY OF THE FIRST WORLD WAR
AND FOCUSED ON EXPLORING AND MANIFESTING THE COMPLEXITIES OF THE
MODERN WORLD IN DIFFERENT WAYS.

ALICE'S ADVENTURES IN WONDERLAND, BY LEWIS CARROLL, HAS AN ICONIC SCENE
IN WHICH ALICE BECOMES CONFUSED ABOUT HER IDENTITY AS HER SIZE CHANGES.
AFTER EATING SOME CAKE, SHE BECOMES TOO LARGE TO FIT ANYWHERE. ALICE
BEGINS TO CRY AND HER GIANT TEARS FORM A POOL. AS SHE CRIES, ALICE SHRINKS
AND FALLS INTO THE POOL OF TEARS, WHICH QUICKLY BECOMES A SEA.

ALICE IS DISTRACTED FROM HER REASON AND REACTS
EMOTIONALLY. THE SEA OF TEARS IS LIKE A PUNISHMENT
FOR ALICE'S GIVING IN TO HER OWN EMOTIONS.

SIGMUND FREUD'S WRITINGS ON THE THEORY OF THE UNCONSCIOUS HAD AN ENORMOUS IMPACT ON MODERNIST LITERATURE. FREUD BELIEVED THAT HUMANS POSSESS A VAST UNCONSCIOUS MIND, FAR GREATER THAN THEIR CONSCIOUS MIND, WHICH IS RESPONSIBLE FOR MANY DIFFERENT HUMAN FEELINGS AND BEHAVIORS.

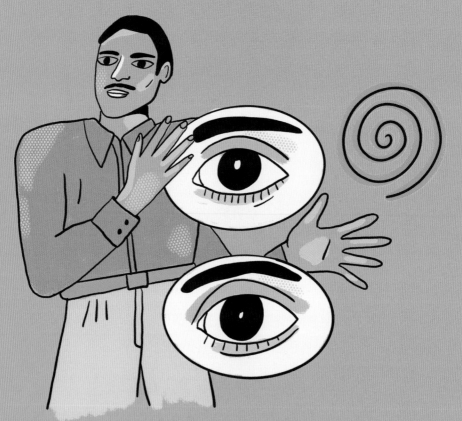

IN HIS WORK *ON THE PSYCHICAL MECHANISM OF HYSTERICAL PHENOMENA*, FREUD EXPRESSED THAT TRAUMATIC MEMORIES, THOUGHT OF AS "FOREIGN BODIES," NEEDED TO BE FLUSHED OUT OF THE PSYCHE. HE VIEWED THE COMBINATION OF TEARS AND WORDS AS DISCHARGE CHANNELS AND RELEASE VALVES.

LITERARY FICTION THAT MAKES US CRY CAN BE VALUABLE FOR VARIOUS REASONS. IT CAN BRING AWARENESS TO A SPECIFIC ISSUE, HELP US EMPATHIZE WITH OTHERS BY OUR UNDERSTANDING HOW GREAT THEIR PAIN IS, TRUMP STEREOTYPES, AND EXPAND OUR VIEW OF THE WORLD. IT CAN ALSO HELP US IDENTIFY AND RELEASE OBSTRUCTIVE EMOTIONS AND ENLARGE OUR CREDENCES AND BELIEFS.

MY OLD FRIEND ROSARIO LET ME BORROW HER COPY OF PATTI SMITH'S BOOK *JUST KIDS* THE SUMMER I WAS TURNING TWENTY-SEVEN. AT THAT TIME, I HAD DECIDED TO SPEND THREE MONTHS IN NEW YORK CITY AFTER A BIG QUARTER-LIFE CRISIS. I WAS FEELING COMPLETELY LOST, AND I THOUGHT I NEEDED TO MOVE 5,295 MILES AWAY FROM HOME TO FIND MY TRUE SELF. I READ THE MEMOIR VORACIOUSLY ON THE PLANE, AND I CRIED ABOUT A WAY OF LIFE THAT NO LONGER EXISTED. I FOUND MYSELF PART OF PATTI SMITH'S STORY. I SPENT THE REST OF MY THREE-MONTH TRIP CRYING AROUND NEW YORK CITY, THINKING ABOUT PATTI SMITH AND ROBERT MAPPLETHORPE.

 SUNDAY, SEPTEMBER 26TH, 2021. I CRIED WATCHING PATTI SMITH PLAY AT THE ELIZABETH STREET GARDEN IN NEW YORK.

I WAS AT THE BEACH WHEN I FINISHED READING *THE YEAR OF MAGICAL THINKING* BY JOAN DIDION. I RAN INTO THE OCEAN AND CRIED UNDERWATER.

THE ART OF CRYING

CRYING AT MUSEUMS IS ONE OF MY FAVORITE ACTIVITIES. VISUAL ARTS CAN MOVE US POWERFULLY, AND THERE IS FASCINATING SCIENTIFIC EVIDENCE ABOUT HOW VIEWING PAINTINGS ACTIVATES THE AREAS OF THE BRAIN THAT ARE RELATED TO INTROSPECTION.

SUNDAY, MARCH 14TH, 2021. I CRIED AT THE MOMA PS1 MUSEUM, STARING AT A PIECE BY NIKI DE SAINT PHALLE.

FOR MY GRANDMOTHER ABA, IT WAS IMPORTANT TO TAKE ME TO A MUSEUM ONCE A WEEK AFTER SCHOOL WHEN I WAS GROWING UP. DURING OUR VISITS TO THE NATIONAL MUSEUM OF FINE ARTS IN BUENOS AIRES, I SOMETIMES CRIED OUT OF BOREDOM AND TIREDNESS. WITH TIME, I LEARNED ABOUT IMPRESSIONISM AND BECAME OBSESSED WITH RODIN'S WORK. NOW, AS SOON AS I SMELL THE SCENT OF STRONG OIL PAINT WHENEVER I VISIT THAT SAME MUSEUM, I CRY, AND NOT JUST BECAUSE OF THE PAINTINGS. I WEEP AS I WALK THROUGH THE GALLERIES, REMEMBERING THOSE GOLDEN AFTERNOONS WITH MY GRANDMOTHER.

THERE IS AN ICONIC PHOTOGRAPH BY THE AVANT-GARDE ARTIST MAN RAY CALLED *TEARS*. HIS STAGED COMPOSITION IS MEANT TO CONVEY THE ARTIFICIALITY OF ART. THE SUBJECT, RESEMBLING A SILENT-SCREEN STAR, STARES UPWARD WHILE SOME BIG, EXAGGERATED TEARDROPS MIMIC A MELODRAMATIC DISPLAY OF SADNESS, SATIRIZING EMOTIONAL EXPRESSION.

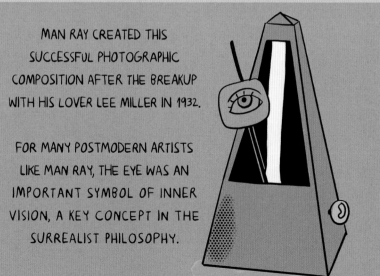

MAN RAY CREATED THIS SUCCESSFUL PHOTOGRAPHIC COMPOSITION AFTER THE BREAKUP WITH HIS LOVER LEE MILLER IN 1932.

FOR MANY POSTMODERN ARTISTS LIKE MAN RAY, THE EYE WAS AN IMPORTANT SYMBOL OF INNER VISION, A KEY CONCEPT IN THE SURREALIST PHILOSOPHY.

IN THE EARLY 1960S, ROY LICHTENSTEIN PRODUCED SEVERAL "FAKE FANTASY DRAMA" PAINTINGS OF WOMEN IN LOVE AFFAIRS WITH HORRIBLE MEN WHO MADE THEM MISERABLE. THESE ORIGINAL ARTWORKS SERVED AS PROLOGUE PAINTINGS TO THE "GIRLS NEXT DOOR" SERIES FROM 1964, WHICH PORTRAYED WOMEN IN A WHOLE ARRAY OF NEBULOUS EMOTIONAL STATES.

DROWNING GIRL, 1963

FRIDA KAHLO'S TEARY SELF-PORTRAIT BROKE THE RECORD AS THE MOST EXPENSIVE LATIN AMERICAN ART PIECE EVER AUCTIONED. THE PAINTING PRESENTS THE MEXICAN ARTIST WITH TEARS IN HER EYES, AND THE FACE OF HER HUSBAND, DIEGO RIVERA, PAINTED ON HER FOREHEAD.

SATURDAY, JANUARY 29TH, 2022. I CRIED ON THE STEPS OF AN IMAGINARY MUSEUM.

CUBAN ARTIST TANIA BRUGUERA CREATED A "CRYING ROOM"
FOR HER EXHIBITION AT LONDON'S TATE MODERN GALLERY
IN 2018. SHE BUILT A SPACE FILLED WITH A
SPECIAL VAPOR DESIGNED TO MAKE PEOPLE WEEP.
BRUGUERA WANTED TO CREATE AN AUTOMATIC
EMPATHIC RESPONSE PRODUCED BY
VISITORS SEEING OTHER PEOPLE CRY.

THIS ROOM
CONTAINS AN
ORGANIC COMPOUND
THAT MAKES
YOU CRY.

SUNDAY, JULY 19TH, 2020. I CRIED AS IF MARINA ABRAMOVIC
WERE LOOKING ME IN THE EYE.

IN HER VISUAL INVESTIGATION *THE TOPOGRAPHY OF TEARS*, PHOTOGRAPHER ROSE-LYNN FISHER CAPTURED TEARS OF JOY, GRIEF, AND IRRITATION IN SUPREME DETAIL. BY USING A STANDARD LIGHT MICROSCOPE AND A MICROSCOPE CAMERA, FISHER TOOK PHOTOS OF DIFFERENT KINDS OF TEARS. EVERY TEAR VISIBLE UNDER THE MICROSCOPIC CAMERA HAD ITS OWN SHAPES AND QUALITIES.

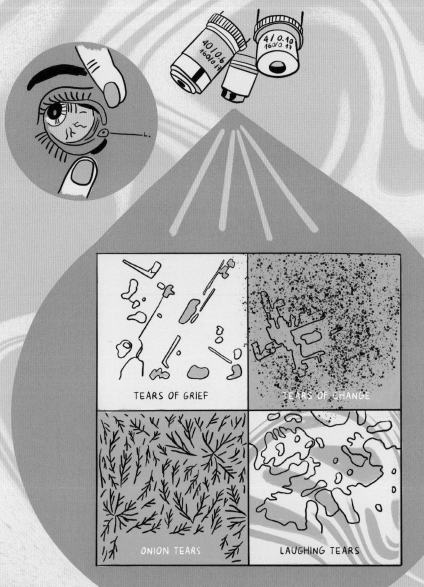

TEARS OF GRIEF

TEARS OF CHANGE

ONION TEARS

LAUGHING TEARS

ART CAN MOVE YOU TO TEARS AND YOUR TEARS ARE A WORK OF ART.

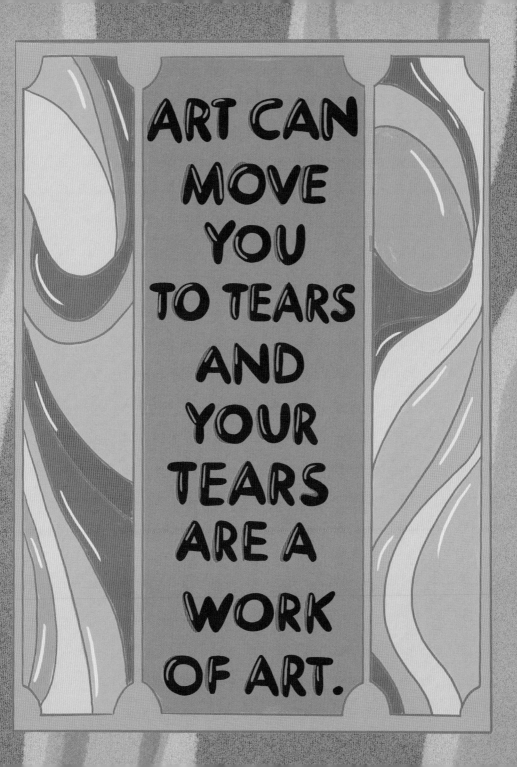

IN THE SUMMER OF 2010, I WAS LIVING IN MILAN, AND I DECIDED TO GET TICKETS TO SEE LEONARDO DA VINCI'S *THE LAST SUPPER*. THE DETERIORATING MURAL, PAINTED WITH TEMPERA AND OIL INSTEAD OF USING STANDARD FRESCO METHODS, REMAINS PROTECTED TO PREVENT FURTHER DAMAGE, AND FEWER THAN A THOUSAND PEOPLE WERE ALLOWED TO VISIT IT EVERY DAY. THE TICKETS PERMIT A FIFTEEN-MINUTE VISIT WITH A MAXIMUM OF TWENTY-FIVE PEOPLE PER TIME SLOT.

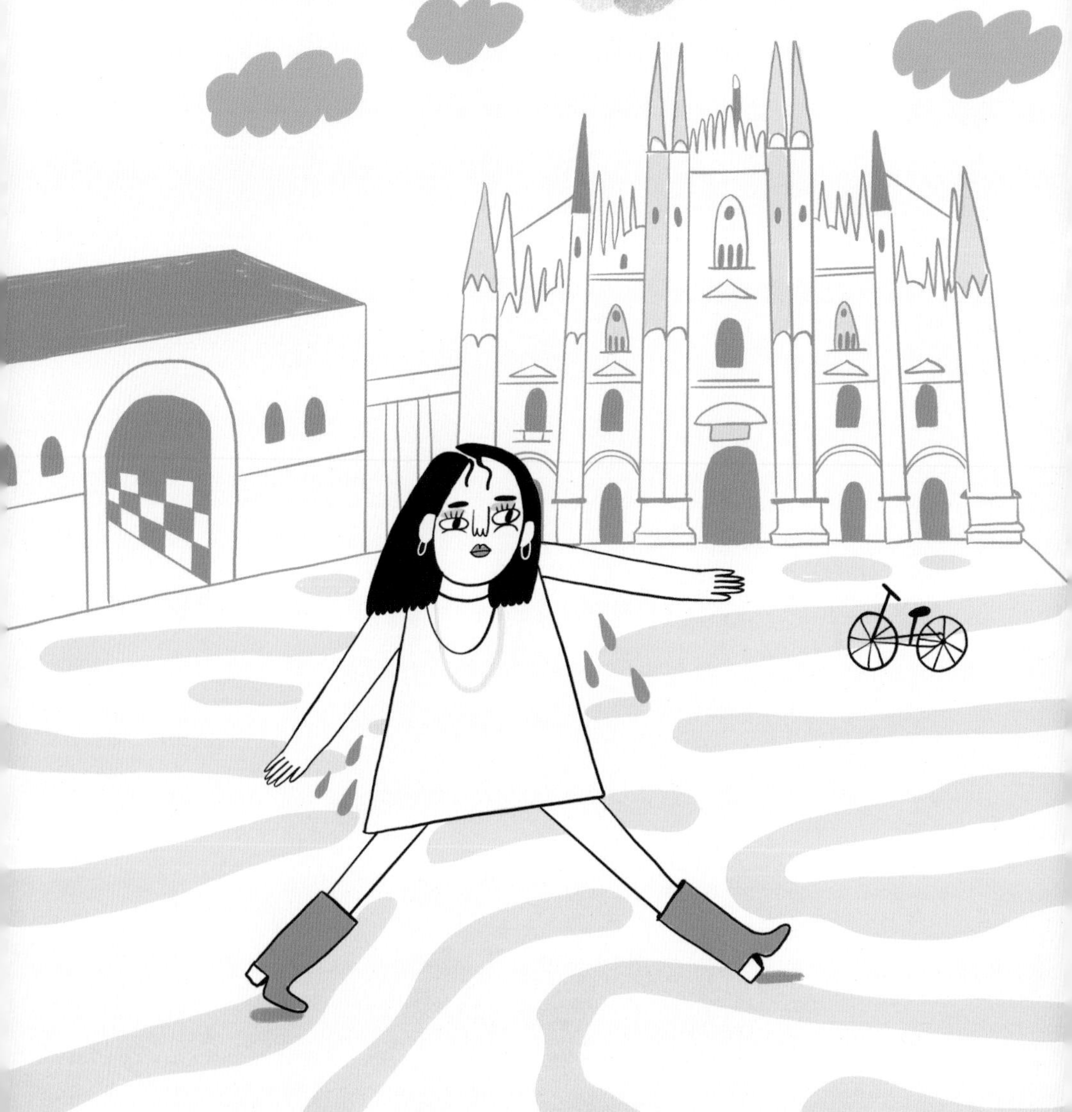

I HAD TO BOOK TICKETS TWO MONTHS IN ADVANCE, AND ON THE DAY OF MY VISIT I DRESSED IN MY FAVORITE WHITE LINEN DRESS AND RODE MY BIKE TO THE ENCOUNTER. HAVING SEEN IMAGES OF THE FAMOUS MURAL ALL MY LIFE, I DIDN'T THINK I WOULD BE OVERLY IMPRESSED AT SEEING IT IN PERSON. I ARRIVED A FEW MINUTES EARLY AT ITS ORIGINAL PLACE, THE FORMER DOMINICAN CONVENT OF SANTA MARIA DELLE GRAZIE.

I WAS ALLOWED INTO A SILENT AND DIMMED ROOM WITH A GROUP OF TWENTY-FOUR STRANGERS. WHEN I FINALLY SAW THE ARTWORK THAT HAD BEEN PAINTED MORE THAN FIVE CENTURIES BEFORE, I WAS MOVED TO TEARS.

THERE WAS SOMETHING ABOUT COMING IN CONTACT WITH AN ICONIC IMAGE, IN A QUIET ROOM WITH UNFAMILIAR PEOPLE, THAT IMPRESSED AND OVERWHELMED ME. THE HUMAN EFFORTS TO KEEP ALIVE A DISAPPEARING PIECE MADE ME CRY FOR THE WHOLE FIFTEEN-MINUTE VISIT.

CRYING CLOWN

THE POPULAR IMAGE OF THE CRYING CLOWN COMES FROM THE 1892 ITALIAN OPERA *PAGLIACCI* BY RUGGERO LEONCAVALLO. ON STAGE, CANIO—THE PROTAGONIST DRESSED AS A CLOWN—IS EXPECTED TO LAUGH EVERYONE'S TROUBLES AWAY; OFF STAGE HE CRIES, TORMENTED WITH THE KNOWLEDGE THAT HIS BEAUTIFUL YOUNG WIFE, NEDDA, IS IN LOVE WITH A HANDSOME SOLDIER.

 MONDAY, NOVEMBER 8TH, 2021. I CRIED FROM EXHAUSTION IN LAS VEGAS, RIGHT IN FRONT OF THE CIRCUS CIRCUS HOTEL.

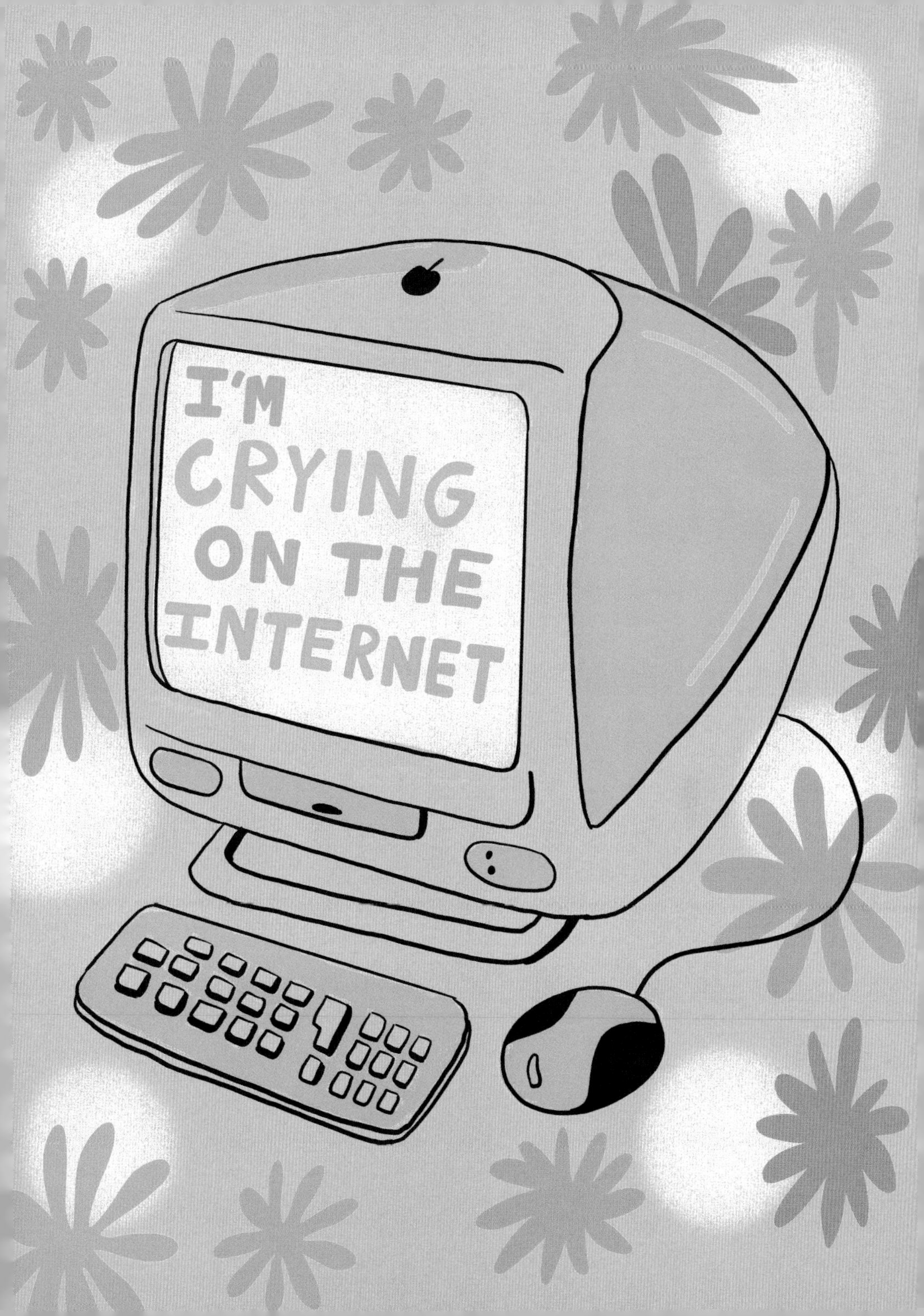
I'M
CRYING
ON THE
INTERNET

IN THE YEAR 2021, SUPERMODEL BELLA HADID POSTED A CRYING SELFIE AND WROTE CANDIDLY ABOUT ONLINE MENTAL HEALTH. AND A NEW CONVERSATION STARTED SURROUNDING SOCIAL MEDIA BREAKDOWNS. CRYING SELFIES BECAME MORE POPULAR, A FORM OF EMOTIONAL CONNECTION AND VALIDATION FROM OTHERS. HOWEVER, SOME SPECIALISTS RECOMMEND TURNING TO THERAPISTS AND MENTAL HEALTH COMMUNITIES, RATHER THAN SPENDING MORE TIME ON SOCIAL MEDIA PLATFORMS.

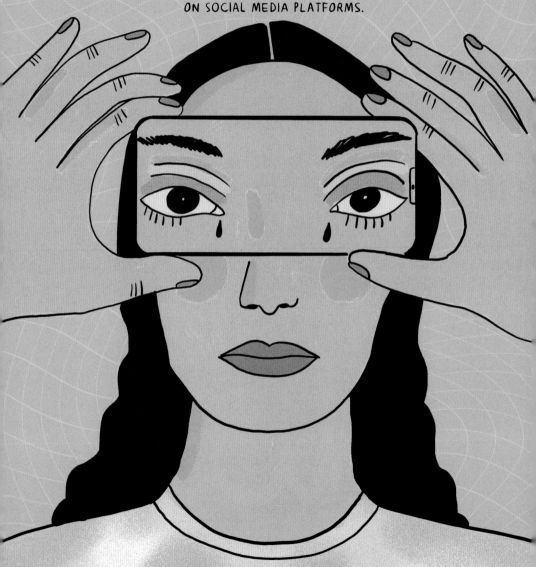

CRYING MEMES

HUMANS LIKE TO SHARE AND REPEAT STUFF. MEMES ARE PIECES OF INFORMATION THAT ARE EXTENSIVELY PASSED FROM ONE INDIVIDUAL TO ANOTHER. BIG CULTURAL SHIFTS CAN BE TRACKED EASILY THROUGH THE DIFFERENT POPULAR MEMES. IN A WORLD WHERE WE ARE SCROLLING THROUGH NEWS FEEDS FOR HOURS AND HOURS EVERY DAY, IT IS NOT A SURPRISE TO SEE WATERFALLS OF CRYING MEMES AS A WAY OF COPING. IT'S AS IF SYMBOLICALLY CRYING ON THE INTERNET IS AN EMOTIONAL RELEASE FOR OUR VIRTUAL SELVES.

 THURSDAY, JULY 30TH, 2020. I CRIED AT A VERY FUNNY MEME.

SINCE THE LAST CENTURY, TEARY GIRLS HAVE BEEN AT THE FOREFRONT OF POPULAR SHOWS AND MOVIES, ONE GREAT EXAMPLE IS SOFIA COPPOLA'S *THE VIRGIN SUICIDES*. WE ALSO SEE THEM IN POP CULTURE ICONS LIKE MARILYN MONROE OR FIONA APPLE. EXACTLY LIKE LANA DEL REY SINGS IN ONE OF HER HIT SONGS: "BECAUSE I'M PRETTY WHEN I CRY."

THE SOFT-CRY LOOK HAS BECOME A POPULAR MAKEUP TREND IN SOCIAL MEDIA CULTURE. SOME CREATORS SHARE TUTORIALS ON HOW TO ACHIEVE A FRESH TEARY LOOK EVEN IF YOU DON'T FEEL LIKE CRYING FOR REAL. IF YOU WANT TO LOOK LIKE YOU ARE "PRETTY CRYING" ALL THE TIME: APPLY PUFFY, SOFT LIPSTICK. THEN PUT SOME RED SHADOW AROUND THE EYES, AND, AS A FINAL TOUCH, DRAW GLITTER EYELINER ALONG THE CHEEKS OF YOUR FACE FOR SOME "CRYING GLOW."

SOMETIMES

YOU JUST HAVE TO PAINT

SOME TEARS ON YOUR FACE

TO FEEL OKAY.

 FRIDAY, JANUARY 20TH, 2023. I FELT LIKE CRYING, AND I PLAYED A MAKEUP TUTORIAL TO DISTRACT MYSELF. I CRIED ALL THE WAY THROUGH.

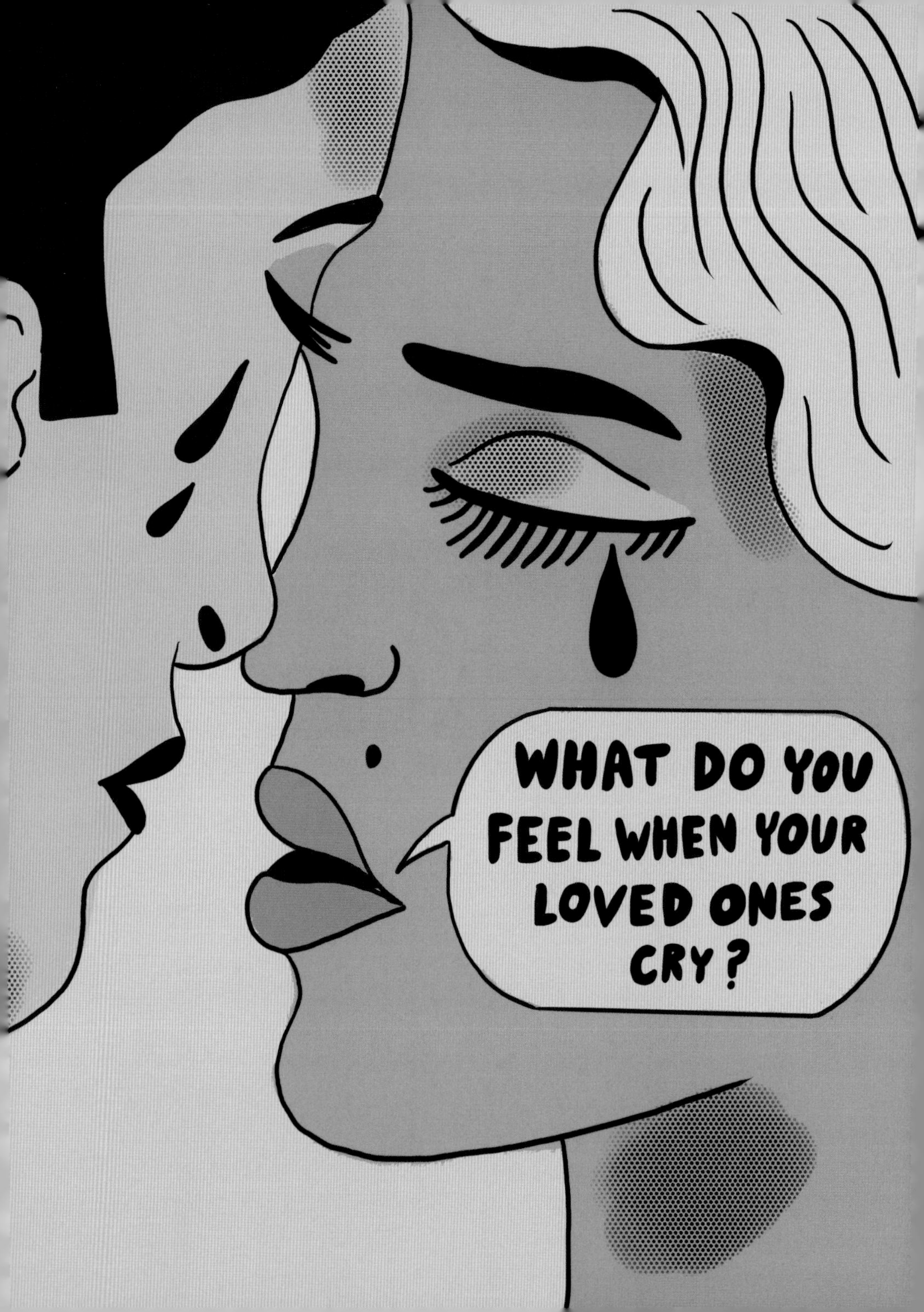
WHAT DO YOU FEEL WHEN YOUR LOVED ONES CRY?

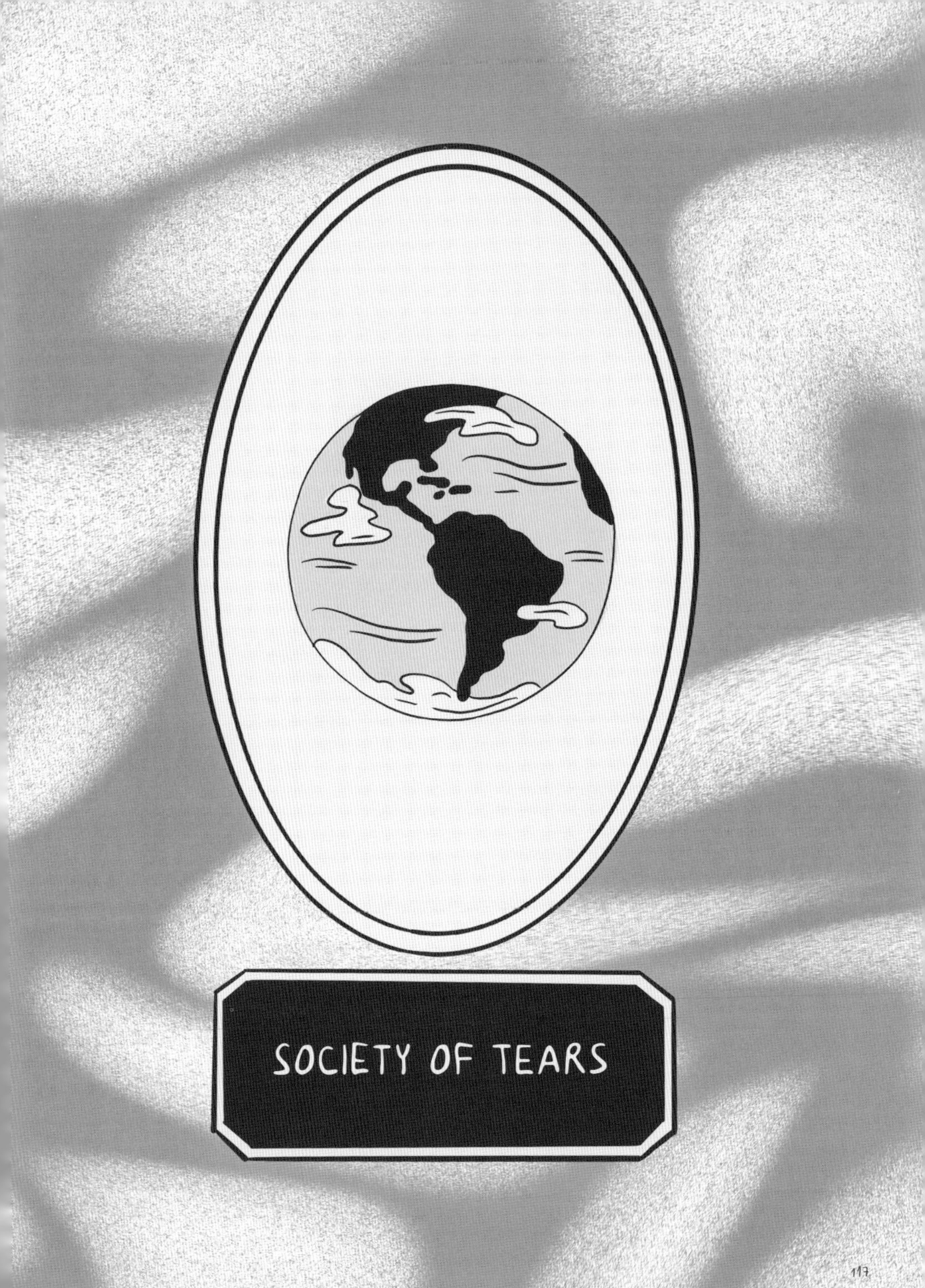
SOCIETY OF TEARS

IT WAS THE YEAR 2000. WE HAD SURVIVED THE Y2K APOCALYPSE, AND THE NEW MILLENNIUM HAD STARTED. I WAS THIRTEEN YEARS OLD, AND ALL I CARED ABOUT WAS CHATTING WITH MY FRIENDS ONLINE. BY THAT TIME, ALMOST EVERY GIRL IN MY CLASS HAD HAD THEIR FIRST PERIOD EXCEPT ME. THIS MADE ME ANXIOUS, BUT AT THE SAME TIME, I WASN'T READY TO GROW UP.

I HAD JUST ARRIVED HOME AFTER PERFORMING IN MY SCHOOL PLAY WHEN I FELT SOME STOMACH PAIN. I RAN TO THE BATHROOM AND SAW SOMETHING RED ON MY UNDERWEAR. I CALLED MY MOM AND CRIED. I KNEW WHAT IT WAS AND WHAT IT MEANT, BUT I DIDN'T WANT MY DAD OR MY BROTHERS TO FIND OUT. I FELT EMBARRASSED AND STUPID AT THE SAME TIME. MY MOM BROUGHT ME A PAD, CALM AS EVER, AND WHISPERED, "THIS IS ONE OF YOUR POWERS."

GENDER ROLES AND TEARS

SOCIETY SHAPES GENDER ROLES AND PLAYS A PART IN HOW HUMANS ENGAGE IN THEIR CRYING EXPERIENCES. ALTHOUGH IT IS BELIEVED THAT WOMEN CRY MORE THAN MEN, THIS DIFFERENCE IS NOT INNATE. DURING CHILDHOOD YEARS, THERE IS LITTLE DISPARITY BETWEEN HOW OFTEN BOYS AND GIRLS CRY.

FROM THE AGE OF ELEVEN DIFFERENCES IN CRYING TENDENCIES AND FREQUENCIES BEGIN TO ARISE BETWEEN ASSIGNED GENDERS. THIS CHANGE IN TEAR PRODUCTION APPEARS TO RESULT FROM A REDUCTION IN MALE TEARS RATHER THAN AN INCREASE IN FEMALE ONES. AT THIS AGE, WOMEN REPORT FEELING BETTER AFTER CRYING, WHILE THEIR MALE PEERS INDICATE THE OPPOSITE.

ON AVERAGE, WOMEN CRY 5.3 TIMES A MONTH, WHILE MEN CRY 1.3 TIMES A MONTH, WITH CRYING DEFINED AS ANYTHING FROM MOIST EYES TO FULL-ON SOBBING.*

BIOLOGICALLY, THERE MAY BE A REASON WHY PEOPLE WITH A UTERUS CRY MORE: TESTOSTERONE MAY INHIBIT CRYING, WHILE THE HORMONE PROLACTIN (SEEN IN HIGHER LEVELS IN MENSTRUATING PEOPLE) MAY PROMOTE IT.

BUT A DESIRE TO CRY IS NOT JUST BIOLOGICAL; IT'S ALSO SOCIOLOGICAL.

THE PATRIARCHY HAS ALWAYS CONTROLLED OUR TEARS.

* DATA WAS FOUND IN THE 1980S BY BIOCHEMIST WILLIAM H. FREY, PHD; THE AVERAGES ARE STILL ABOUT THE SAME TODAY, ACCORDING TO LAUREN BYLSMA, PHD, OF THE UNIVERSITY OF PITTSBURGH AND OTHERS.

PREMENSTRUAL SYNDROME

MENSTRUATION AND OVULATION CREATE HORMONAL FLUCTUATIONS THROUGHOUT THE MONTH. EXPERTS BELIEVE THAT THE DROP IN ESTROGEN AND PROGESTERONE, WHICH OCCURS AFTER OVULATION, IS A TRIGGER FOR CRYING. THESE HORMONES REDUCE PRODUCTION OF SEROTONIN, A CHEMICAL NEUROTRANSMITTER SOMETIMES REFERRED TO AS ONE OF THE "HAPPINESS" CHEMICALS. CRYING BEFORE AND DURING THE FIRST FEW DAYS OF THE MENSTRUAL PERIOD IS VERY COMMON AND CAN BE CAUSED BY A WHOLE ARRAY OF CHANGING EMOTIONS. ONE MINUTE YOU'RE SAD, THE NEXT YOU'RE CHEERFUL AND ENERGIZED. HORMONES CAN ALSO CREATE THE URGE TO CRY, EVEN IF IT FEELS LIKE THERE'S NO REASON FOR IT.

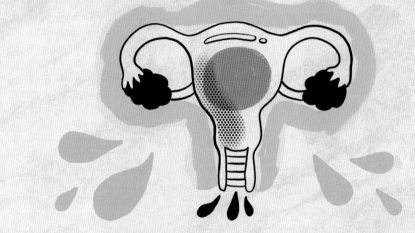

WAYS TO COPE WITH PMS:

* EAT FOODS HIGH IN OMEGA-3 FATTY ACIDS, SUCH AS FISH AND WALNUTS.
* IF POSSIBLE, EXERCISE. THIS WILL TRIGGER THE RELEASE OF ENDORPHINS, WHICH IN TURN WILL HELP IMPROVE YOUR MOOD.
* DO SOMETHING FUN TO DISTRACT YOURSELF FROM CHANGING EMOTIONS.
* HAVE A GOOD CRY.

AT SOME POINT IN OUR RELATIONSHIP, EVERY ROMANTIC PARTNER I'VE EVER HAD HAS ASKED ME WHY I CRY SO MUCH, AND I HAVE ASKED WHY THEY DIDN'T. THE RESPONSE LIES IN THE SOCIALIZATION OF WOMEN TO CRY INSTEAD OF EXPRESSING THEIR ANGER, WHEREAS CISGENDER MEN ARE CONDITIONED TO DISPLAY ANGER WHEN THEY MIGHT ACTUALLY FEEL LIKE CRYING.

 THURSDAY, JANUARY 26TH, 2023. I CRIED BECAUSE I SAW MY PARTNER CRYING WHILE LISTENING TO A PODCAST.

HOW WE TEACH CHILDREN TO EXPRESS EMOTIONS
CAN HAVE A BIG IMPACT ON HOW THEY FEEL AND BEHAVE.
BOYS ARE OFTEN TAUGHT TO HIDE THEIR SADNESS AND
EXPRESS ANGER INSTEAD, WHILE GIRLS ARE ENCOURAGED TO DO THE
OPPOSITE. THESE PATTERNS CAN BE REINFORCED BY THEIR PEERS, ESPECIALLY
IN CULTURES IN WHICH EMOTIONAL DIFFERENCES BETWEEN GENDER ARE
EMPHASIZED. THIS IS APPARENT IN THE WELL-KNOWN SAYING "BOYS DON'T CRY."

DURING THE TWENTIETH CENTURY, PATRIARCHAL MAINSTREAM CULTURE EMPHASIZED THE NOTION THAT EMOTIONS WERE A FORM OF WEAKNESS.

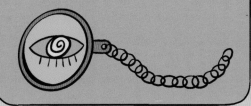

CRYING WOMEN WERE SEEN AS DEMANDING, WHEREAS A CERTAIN AMOUNT OF TEARS FROM MEN WERE CONSIDERED A COMPLIMENT. (IT SHOWED THAT THOSE MEN CARED.)

IN THE '60s THE NOTION THAT WOMEN WERE MORE "EMOTIONAL" AND MEN MORE "RATIONAL" WAS CEMENTED AS A SEXIST IDEOLOGY.

LA LLORONA

THE MEXICAN FOLK FIGURE LA LLORONA, WHOSE NAME MEANS "WEEPING WOMAN," IS A WOMAN WHO HAUNTS THE WOODS AND RIVERS AT NIGHT, LOOKING FOR SMALL CHILDREN. THE MOST TERRIFYING THING ABOUT HER IS THAT SHE IS A WOMAN WHO WEEPS FOREVER. "BE GOOD OR LA LLORONA WILL COME AND GET YOU," WARN PARENTS, SO THAT THEIR CHILDREN WILL BE ON THEIR BEST BEHAVIOR FOR FEAR OF BEING TAKEN AWAY.

THERE ARE MANY DIFFERENT VARIATIONS TO THE STORY. SOME PROMOTE THE IDEA OF A WOMAN WHO DOESN'T RESPECT HER HUSBAND'S WISHES AND, AS A RESULT, IS CONDEMNED TO SUFFER FOREVER.

FEMINISTS IN THE '60S CHALLENGED THE IDEA THAT EMOTIONS WERE SOLELY THE DOMAIN OF WOMEN AND REASON THE DOMAIN OF MEN, AND ADVOCATED FOR CREATING A MORE HOLISITIC UNDERSTANDING OF HUMAN EXPERIENCE THAT INCLUDED BOTH. SOME FEMINISTS CLAIMED THAT EMOTION WAS THE ULTIMATE HUMAN RESPONSE AND THAT THE RATIONAL MIND WAS ONLY A PART OF THE CRYING EXPERIENCE.

GLORIA STEINEM ONCE SAID THAT SHE CRIES WHENEVER SHE GETS TOO ANGRY.

TO PUSH BACK ON HER CRYING BEING PERCEIVED BY MEN AS A WEAKNESS, SHE PROPOSED SAYING TO THEM:

"THIS IS HOW I GET ANGRY. I AM CRYING BECAUSE I'M ANGRY. BECAUSE I AM CRYING, I WILL LIVE LONGER THAN YOU."

CRYING IN PUBLIC IS A FEMINIST ACT.

IN 2015, AFTER THE FOURTH WAVE OF FEMINISM EMERGED GLOBALLY, THE NI UNA MENOS MOVEMENT WAS FOUNDED IN ARGENTINA. THAT YEAR, WE STARTED MARCHING IN THE STREETS, ASKING FOR JUSTICE ON A MASSIVE SCALE. AT THE TIME, MORE FEMICIDES WERE OCCURRING EVERY DAY. WE CRIED AND CRIED FOR THESE WOMEN'S DEATHS. WE CRIED TOGETHER FOR DAYS AND NIGHTS, FOR OUR SISTERS AND THEIR LOST VOICES. WE CRIED BECAUSE THEY COULD NOT CRY ANYMORE.

 WEDNESDAY, DECEMBER 30TH, 2020. I CRIED ALL DAY, BECAUSE AFTER A FEW YEARS OF STRUGGLE, ABORTION BECAME LEGAL IN ARGENTINA.

I CAN'T BELIEVE

WE STILL HAVE TO

EXPLAIN

WE ARE ALSO

HUMAN BEINGS

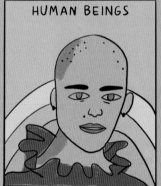

LIVING ON THE SAME

PLANET

AND THAT WE NEED

EQUAL RIGHTS.

FOR MANY TRANS PEOPLE, CRYING MEANS THEY CAN EXPRESS THEMSELVES FREELY AND BE COMFORTABLE WITH WHO THEY REALLY ARE. BEING INSIDE A BODY THAT DOESN'T FEEL LIKE YOUR OWN CAN SOMETIMES LEAD TO REPRESSED EMOTIONS. GENDER TRANSITION AND HORMONE REPLACEMENT THERAPY CAN OPEN A WHOLE NEW RANGE OF FEELINGS, ESPECIALLY AFTER YEARS OF BEING MISGENDERED.

TRANS WOMEN AND MEN OFTEN DISCOVER THE EMOTIONAL BENEFIT OF THEIR TRANSITION NOT SO MUCH BY DISCOVERING A NEW WAY OF FEELING BUT BY FINALLY FEELING WHAT HAS ALWAYS EXISTED WITHIN THEM. THEY RECOGNIZE THAT FEELINGS ARE MORE AVAILABLE TO THEM, INSTEAD OF BURIED IN DEEP-ROOTED LAYERS OF GENDER DYSPHORIA. SOME HAVE FOUND THAT THEY ALLOW THEMSELVES TO FEEL A WHOLE ARRAY OF EMOTIONS, IN PART BECAUSE THEY NO LONGER SPEND SO MUCH TIME HATING THEIR PHYSICAL SELVES.

CRYING WHILE PREGNANT

CHANGES IN MOOD AND SUDDEN CRYING SPELLS ARE AN EXPECTED PART OF GESTATION; IT TAKES SOME TIME TO ABSORB THE EMOTIONAL WEIGHT AND THE SIGNIFICANT TRANSFORMATIONS INVOLVED IN CARRYING A CHILD.

CHANGES IN EMOTIONS CAN OFTEN BE ATTRIBUTED TO HORMONAL FLUCTUATIONS, WHICH HAVE THE ABILITY TO AFFECT THE BRAIN'S CHEMICAL BALANCE AND REGULATE MOOD. A PREGNANT PERSON'S EMOTIONAL WELL-BEING AND MENTAL HEALTH ARE JUST AS IMPORTANT AS THEIR PHYSICAL HEALTH. CRYING CAN BE A HELPFUL MECHANISM IN MANAGING MENTAL HEALTH DURING PREGNANCY.

"TINY TEARS"—THE DOLL THAT CRIES REAL TEARS.

GIVE YOUR LITTLE GIRL A DOLL TO LOVE—A DOLL SO REAL, SO HUMAN, THAT SHE WILL BE KEPT BUSY AND HAPPY DAY AFTER DAY.

TINY TEARS DRINKS HER BOTTLE, WETS HER DIAPER, BLOWS BUBBLES, SLEEPS, CAN BE BATHED, AND MOST WONDERFUL OF ALL: WHEN SHE CRIES, BIG WET TEARS FALL DOWN HER CHUBBY CHEEKS.

THERE'S NO OTHER DOLL IN THE WORLD LIKE HER.

 TUESDAY, APRIL 26TH, 2022. I CRIED BECAUSE A CHILDHOOD MEMORY CROSSED MY MIND IN THE MIDDLE OF THE DAY.

CRYING DOLLS BECAME POPULAR DURING THE 1950S AND WERE AIMED AT LITTLE GIRLS. DECADES OF GENDER STEREOTYPING CONSUMPTION HAVE LED US TO BELIEVE THAT BOYS WEAR BLUE, HAVE SHORT HAIR, AND PLAY WITH CARS, WHILE GIRLS LIKE PINK, PLAY WITH DOLLS, AND CRY MORE FREQUENTLY.

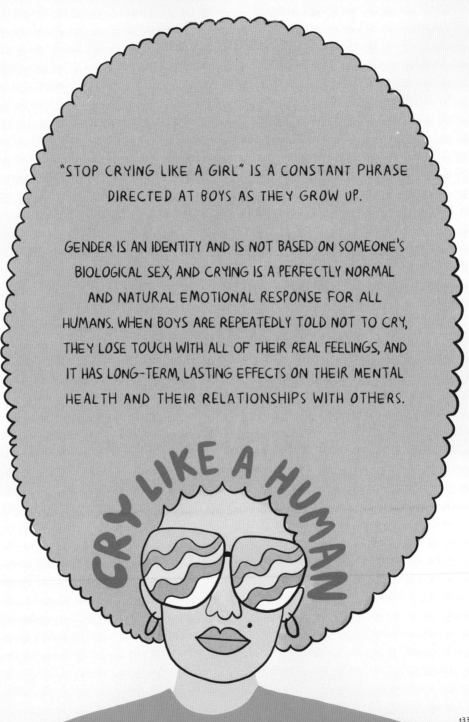

"STOP CRYING LIKE A GIRL" IS A CONSTANT PHRASE DIRECTED AT BOYS AS THEY GROW UP.

GENDER IS AN IDENTITY AND IS NOT BASED ON SOMEONE'S BIOLOGICAL SEX, AND CRYING IS A PERFECTLY NORMAL AND NATURAL EMOTIONAL RESPONSE FOR ALL HUMANS. WHEN BOYS ARE REPEATEDLY TOLD NOT TO CRY, THEY LOSE TOUCH WITH ALL OF THEIR REAL FEELINGS, AND IT HAS LONG-TERM, LASTING EFFECTS ON THEIR MENTAL HEALTH AND THEIR RELATIONSHIPS WITH OTHERS.

CRY LIKE A HUMAN

CRYING AROUND THE WORLD

ACROSS VARIOUS CULTURES, WOMEN TEND TO CRY MORE FREQUENTLY AND HAVE MORE POSITIVE CRYING EXPERIENCES. SOME STUDIES PROPOSE THAT SOCIO-CULTURAL FACTORS MIGHT PLAY A SIGNIFICANT ROLE IN SHAPING THE EXPRESSION OF CRYING.

DATA COLLECTED FROM THIRTY-SEVEN COUNTRIES SUGGESTS THAT IN WEALTHIER NATIONS BOTH MEN AND WOMEN FEEL BETTER AFTER CRYING THAN IN COUNTRIES WITH LESS EQUALITY AND WEALTH. THE GENDER GAP IN RICHER NATIONS IS NARROWER AND PEOPLE REPORT SHEDDING TEARS MORE OFTEN WITHOUT PITY OR SHAME.

TEARS ARE DIAMONDS

FOR A LONG TIME, IT WAS THOUGHT THAT PEOPLE IN DEVELOPED COUNTRIES
WERE COLDER AND REPRESSED THEIR EMOTIONS, BUT NEW RESEARCH HAS
FOUND THAT AS SOCIETIES GET RICHER, PEOPLE CRY MORE AND MORE.
WHILE RESEARCHERS WOULD HAVE ASSUMED THAT INDIVIDUALS IN LESS
AFFLUENT COUNTRIES WOULD HAVE MORE REASONS FOR CRYING, THEY FOUND
THAT IT WAS PEOPLE IN WEALTHIER COUNTRIES WHO REPORTED CRYING MORE
OFTEN. THE VARIABLES THAT CORRELATED WITH CRYING MORE FREQUENTLY
WERE THE LEVELS OF CIVIL RIGHTS, DEMOCRACY, AND ALSO INDIVIDUAL EXPRESSION.
INTERNATIONALLY, CRYING SEEMS TO BE MORE RELATED TO A CERTAIN
FREEDOM TO EXPRESS EMOTION RATHER THAN SOCIAL DISTRESS.

CRYING ON THE JOB

I DON'T THINK I'M EXAGGERATING WHEN I SAY I HAVE CRIED AT EVERY JOB I'VE EVER HAD. WHEN I WAS TWENTY-TWO, AT MY FIRST CREATIVE JOB AT A FASHION BRAND, I WOULD SAVE FABRIC SAMPLES TO DRY MY TEARS BEFORE MEETINGS.

TEARS AT WORK HAVE LONG BEEN DISCOURAGED. PEOPLE WHO CRY RISK BEING PERCEIVED AS LESS PROFESSIONAL THAN THEIR MORE IMPERTURBABLE COWORKERS.

 SATURDAY, JULY 9TH, 2022. I CRIED BECAUSE I FINALLY SIGNED THE CONTRACT WITH A PUBLISHER FOR THE CRYING BOOK I'VE BEEN WORKING ON FOR THE PAST FEW YEARS.

FOR POLITICIANS, CRYING HAS ALWAYS BEEN CONSIDERED A SIGN OF WEAKNESS. SOCIETY TENDS TO PREFER LEADERS WHO APPEAR CONFIDENT, UNFLAPPABLE, AND SELF-ASSURED, AND CRYING HAS LONG BEEN SEEN AS A SYMBOL OF VULNERABILITY. PERSONALLY, I PREFER MY CANDIDATES CRYING RATHER THAN UNFEELING.

HOWEVER, SOME BREAKDOWNS ARE SIGNS OF HUMAN KINDNESS IN POLITICS, LIKE CRYING DURING A PANDEMIC, A GLOBAL CRISIS, OR A NATIONAL TRAGEDY.

 MONDAY, DECEMBER 28TH, 2020. I CRIED WATCHING THE SENATORS DEBATE IN BUENOS AIRES.

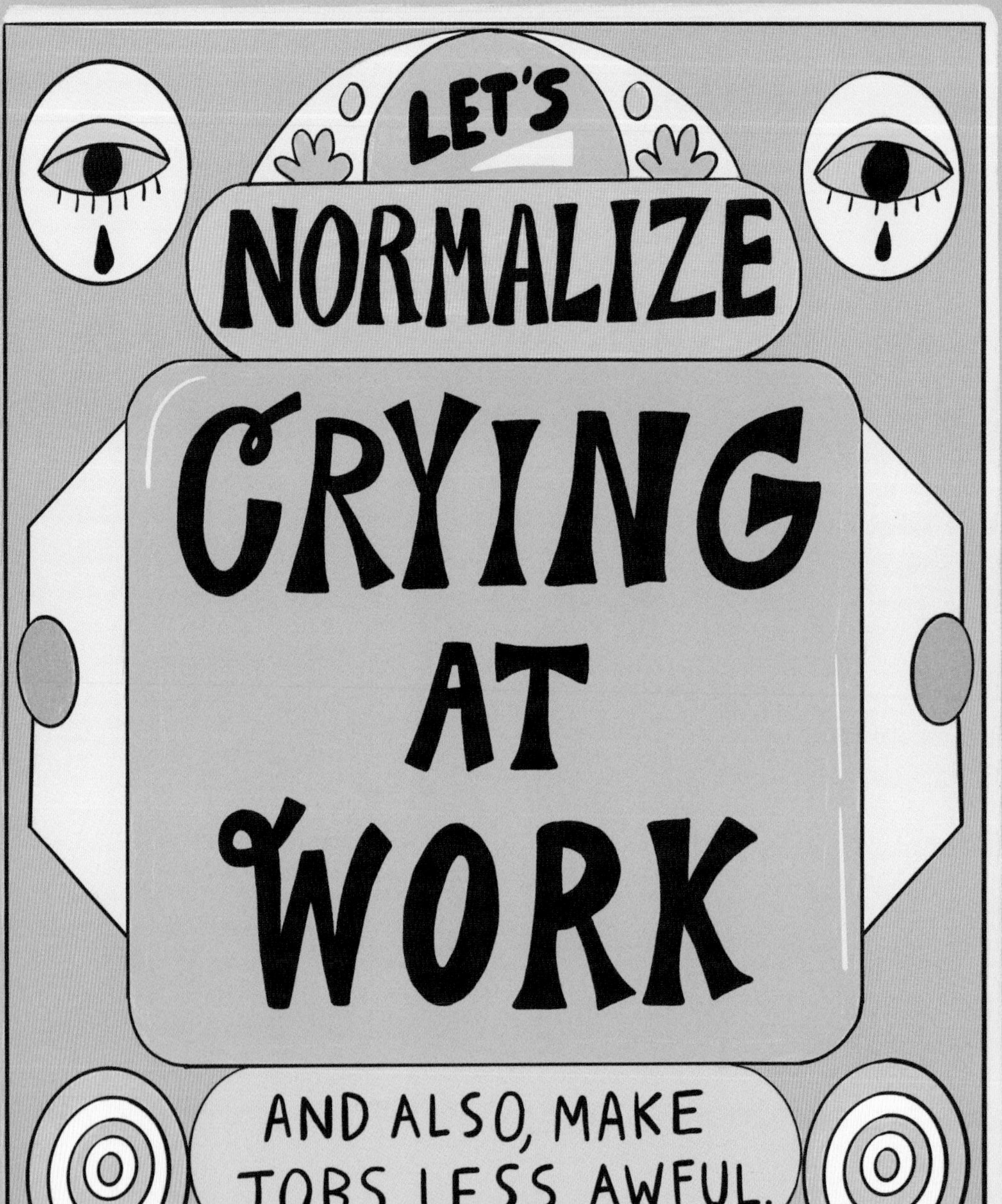
LET'S
NORMALIZE
CRYING
AT
WORK
AND ALSO, MAKE
JOBS LESS AWFUL.

SOME DOCTORS, ESPECIALLY SURGEONS, MAINTAIN THAT CRYING IN FRONT OF A PATIENT IS CONSIDERED A SIGN OF WEAKNESS AND A LACK OF PROFESSIONAL EXPERIENCE. ON THE OTHER HAND, NURSES OFTEN FEEL THAT THEY CAN EXPRESS MORE EMOTION. SHOWING PATIENTS THAT THEY ARE HUMANS WHO CARE, AND ALSO HAVE FEELINGS, CAN BREAK THROUGH THE COLDNESS OF HOSPITAL ENVIRONMENTS.

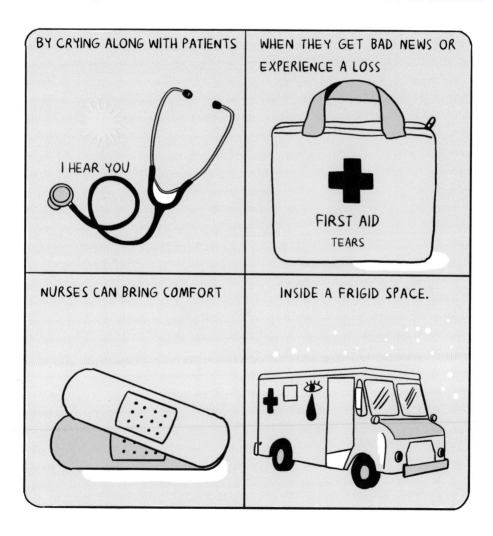

BY CRYING ALONG WITH PATIENTS

I HEAR YOU

WHEN THEY GET BAD NEWS OR EXPERIENCE A LOSS

FIRST AID
TEARS

NURSES CAN BRING COMFORT

INSIDE A FRIGID SPACE.

WHEN I WAS FINISHING HIGH SCHOOL, MY MOTHER WAS DIAGNOSED WITH BREAST CANCER. I REMEMBER TEARING UP WITH HER WHEN SHE TOLD ME THE TERRIFYING NEWS. I CRIED IN THE HOSPITAL WHILE SHE WAS BEING TAKEN INTO SURGERY. I WAS SITTING IN A FEATURELESS, STERILE CORNER, ALL CURLED UP. I SOBBED, WATCHING DOCTORS MOVE LIKE ROBOTS THROUGH THE ASEPTIC HALLWAYS. I SAT THERE SECRETLY WISHING SOMEONE WOULD HUG ME.

WHEN MY MOM FINALLY RECOVERED, AND HER TESTS ASSURED US SHE WAS CANCER-FREE, I CRIED AGAIN WITH HAPPINESS IN THE SAME WHITE CORNER.

BY ASSIGNING A SPECIFIC GENDER TO CERTAIN EMOTIONS, SOCIETIES MAINTAIN THE FALSE IDEA THAT WOMEN ARE ALWAYS, NATURALLY AND BIOLOGICALLY, ABLE TO FEEL, EXPRESS, AND MANAGE EMOTIONS BETTER THAN MEN.

THE TERM "EMOTIONAL LABOR" WAS FIRST EXPRESSED BY SOCIOLOGIST ARLIE HOCHSCHILD IN HER 1979 BOOK, *THE MANAGED HEART*. THE TERM REFERS TO UNPAID LABOR THAT IS UNDERTAKEN TO MANAGE EMOTIONS— YOUR OWN AND OTHERS'—BOTH AT A JOB AND AT HOME, AND IS DISPROPORTIONATELY PERFORMED BY WOMEN.

EMOTIONAL LABOR CAN BE JUST AS DEMANDING AS PHYSICAL LABOR, ESPECIALLY WHEN IT REQUIRES SHUTTING DOWN PERSONAL FEELINGS TO MEET THE EMOTIONAL NEEDS OF OTHER PEOPLE. FEMALE WORKERS ARE EXPECTED TO CARE FOR THE CHANGING EMOTIONS OF THE PEOPLE THEY ARE ASSISTING.

MONETARY COMPENSATION IN SERVICE INDUSTRIES IN WHICH WOMEN ARE PREDOMINANTLY EMPLOYED IS FAR LOWER THAN IN MALE-DOMINATED INDUSTRIES.

FEELING CHARTS ARE HELPFUL FOR ALL CHILDREN AND EVEN ADULTS WHO HAVE TROUBLE NAMING AND IDENTIFYING FEELINGS. WHEN WE ARE HAVING A PARTICULAR SENTIMENT, THE CHART HELPS US RECOGNIZE THAT EMOTION AND CRY IF NEEDED.

HOW ARE YOU FEELING TODAY?

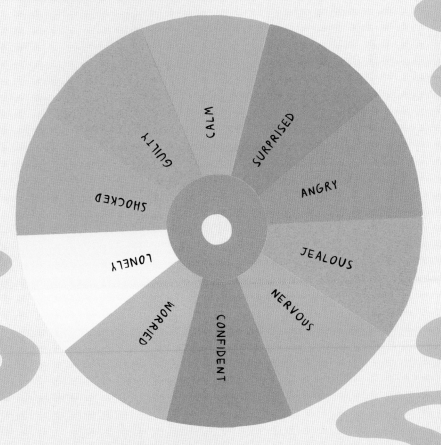

CRYING TAKES PRACTICE

HIDEFUMI YOSHIDA IS A SELF-DESCRIBED TEARS TEACHER WHO TRAVELS ACROSS JAPAN TO ENCOURAGE ADULTS TO CRY MORE. HE PROCLAIMS THAT CRYING THERAPY IS A WAY TO DETOXIFY THE MIND BY FORCING YOURSELF TO SHED TEARS EVEN FOR JUST A FEW MINUTES EVERY MONTH.

IN A SOCIETY WHERE HOLDING BACK TEARS IS CONSIDERED A VIRTUE, HE WANTS PEOPLE TO RELEASE ALL THAT TENSION THROUGH THIS EMOTIVE RESPONSE.

"THE ACT OF CRYING IS MORE EFFECTIVE THAN LAUGHING OR SLEEPING IN REDUCING STRESS. IF YOU CRY ONCE A WEEK, YOU CAN LIVE A STRESS-FREE LIFE," SAYS YOSHIDA.

 WEDNESDAY, MAY 5TH, 2021. I CRIED DURING A VIRTUAL GYM CLASS.

MR. YOSHIDA MAKES PATIENTS CRY BY HAVING THEM WATCH VIDEOS, LISTEN TO SONGS, VIEW PICTURE BOOKS, AND SHARE STORIES. HIS WORKSHOPS CONSIST OF FIVE STEPS.

1. WATCH INSPIRING VIDEOS
IN THIS FIRST STEP, YOSHIDA SHOWS THE CLASS EMOTIONAL VIDEOS. HE OBSERVES THAT EVERYONE HAS A DIFFERENT CRYING POINT IN EACH VIDEO AND THE TRIGGER POINT FOR TEARS HAS SOMETHING TO DO WITH EACH INDIVIDUAL'S PAST EXPERIENCE. THE VIDEOS SCREENED ARE NOT LIMITED TO FAMILY LOVE OR HUMAN LIFE AND DEATH. EVERY VIDEO HAS MANY ASPECTS THAT QUESTION WHAT MAKES STRENGTH, KINDNESS, AND WARMTH.

2. USE WORDS TO RELEASE STRESS
STUDENTS WRITE A "CRYING WORD" ON A TEAR-SHAPED PAPER AND SUBMIT IT TO THE INSTRUCTOR. THE TEACHER WILL GIVE ADVICE BASED ON THE WORD AND EXPLAIN HOW TEARS CAN BE USEFUL FOR EACH SPECIFIC STUDENT.

3. CREATE A CRYING STORY
PARTICIPANTS BECOME SPEAKERS AND LISTENERS AND SHARE CRYING STORIES WITH ONE ANOTHER TO ENHANCE EMPATHY. THE FEEDBACK EVERYONE GETS MAY REMIND THEM HOW HELPFUL IT CAN BE TO SHARE TEARS.

4. LISTEN TO A LECTURE ABOUT TEARS
THE INSTRUCTOR GIVES A LECTURE ON THE EFFECTS OF TEARS.

5. TALK WITH EVERYONE
PEOPLE SHARE THEIR CRYING EXPERIENCES AND INTERACT WITH ONE ANOTHER. THEY EXCHANGE OPINIONS ABOUT WHERE THEY CRIED, WHY THEY CRIED, OR WHY THEY DID NOT CRY.

THE WHOLE EXPERIENCE CAN BE AN OPPORTUNITY TO THINK ABOUT WHERE EVERYONE IS IN THEIR OWN LIFE.

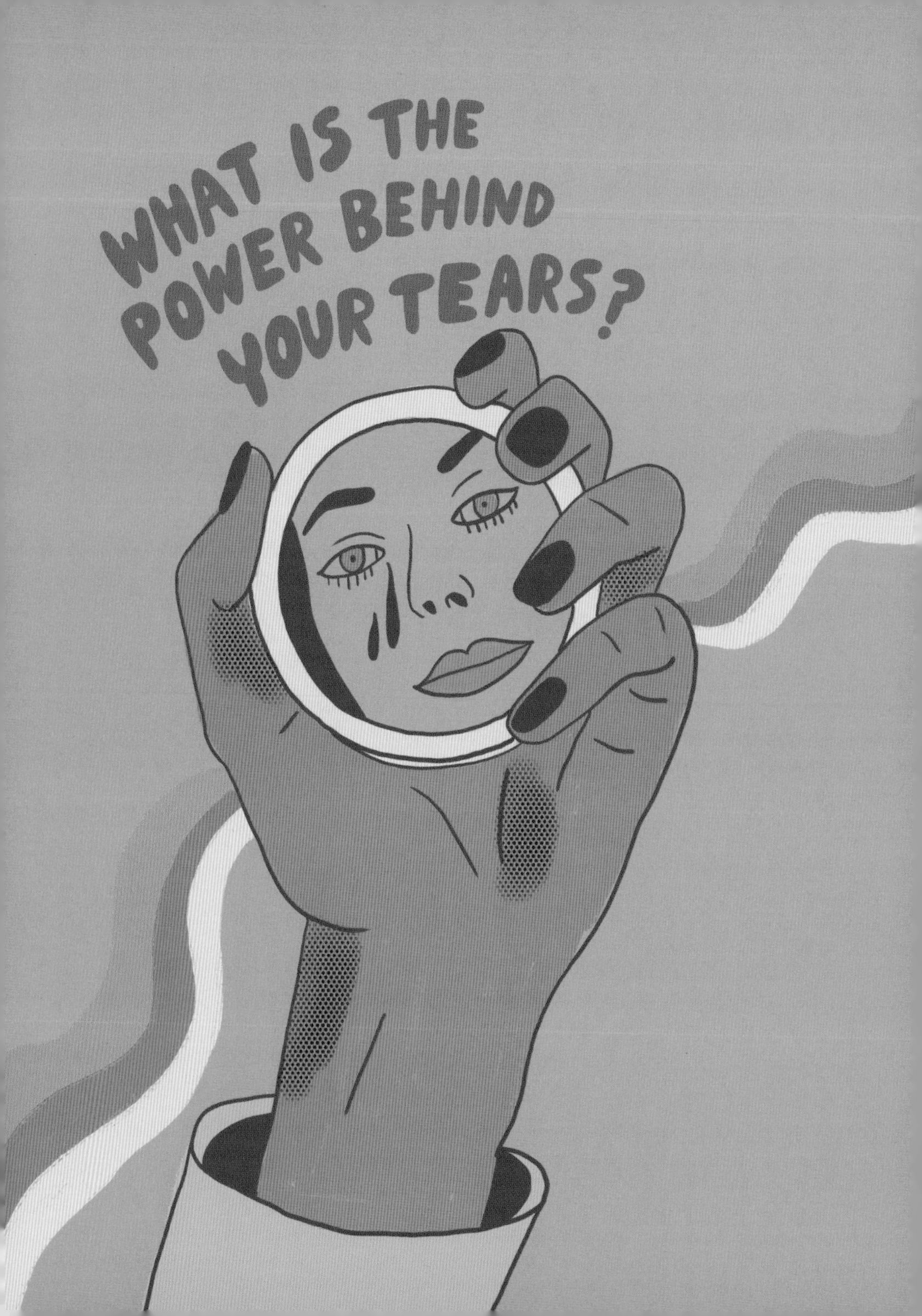
WHAT IS THE
POWER BEHIND
YOUR TEARS?

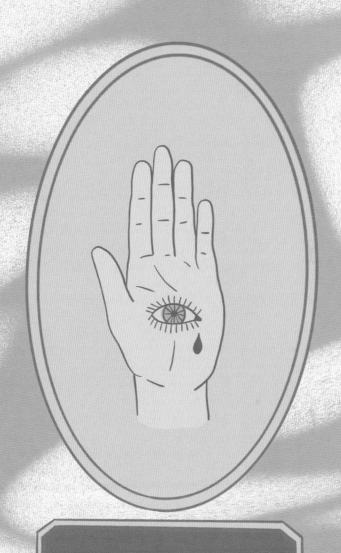

EXISTENTIAL TEARS

CRYING HAS A PURPOSE: HUMAN TEARS HAVE ALWAYS BEEN A PART OF EVOLUTION, HELPING US ADAPT TO NEW REALITIES. THERE'S NO POINT IN HOLDING THEM INSIDE. TEARS LUBRICATE LIFE, BIRTH, AND DEATH. CRYING IS PART OF VISIBLE PUBLIC ACTS OF LOVE AND PRIVATE EXPRESSIONS OF PAIN.

 MONDAY, SEPTEMBER 12TH, 2022. I CRIED CLEANING THE OVEN AND FELT READY FOR THE NEXT STAGE OF MY LIFE.

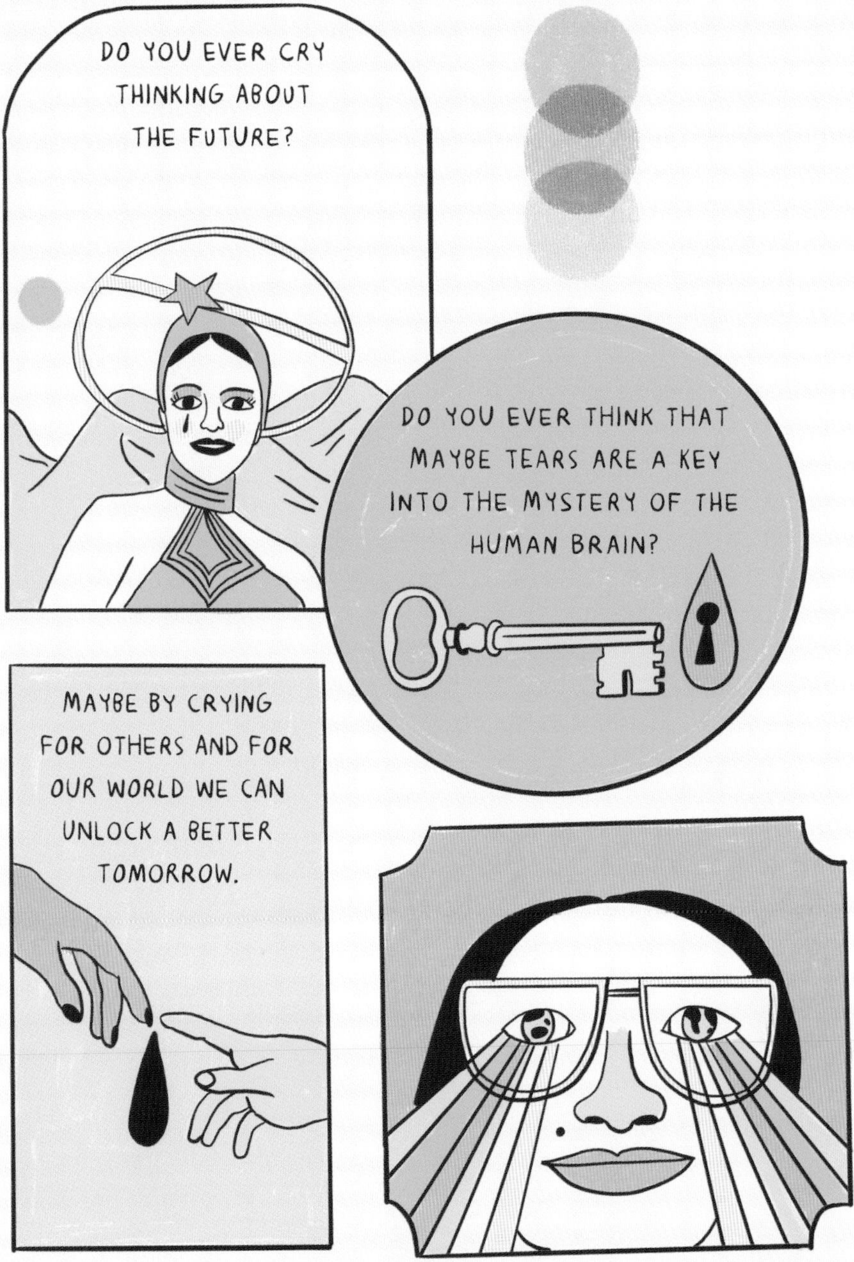
DO YOU EVER CRY THINKING ABOUT THE FUTURE?
DO YOU EVER THINK THAT MAYBE TEARS ARE A KEY INTO THE MYSTERY OF THE HUMAN BRAIN?
MAYBE BY CRYING FOR OTHERS AND FOR OUR WORLD WE CAN UNLOCK A BETTER TOMORROW.

CRYING IN DREAMS

SOME DREAM SPECIALISTS SUGGEST THAT WAKING UP CRYING FROM A DREAM HAPPENS WHEN YOUR UNCONSCIOUS MIND FINALLY TOUCHES UPON SOME DEEPLY BURIED GRIEF. WHEN YOU AWAKE CRYING, IT IS GOOD AND HEALING. WHETHER OR NOT YOU REMEMBER WHAT THE DREAM WAS ABOUT, TEARS ARE BETTER OUTSIDE THAN INSIDE YOUR BODY.

SOME DREAM EXPERTS SAY THAT CRYING IN DREAMS REPRESENTS FORGIVENESS AND OLD FEELINGS BEING WASHED AWAY. YOU MIGHT FEEL ALMOST RESTORED AND REJUVENATED WHEN YOU WAKE UP FROM SLEEP.

 SUNDAY, JUNE 5TH, 2022. I WOKE UP FROM MY SLEEP, AND I WAS CRYING REAL TEARS.

DURING THE FIRST MONTH OF THE COVID-19 PANDEMIC, I HAD LUCID DREAMS EVERY NIGHT. I THINK I WENT INTO SURVIVAL MODE. IN MY LOCKDOWN DREAMS, I CRIED AND HUGGED MY MOM AND MY GRANDMOTHER. I FELT THE TEXTURE AND SMELL OF THEIR CLOTHES.

SOMETIMES TEARS IN DREAMS HELP ME NAVIGATE UNPREDICTABLE WATERS IN REAL LIFE.

DURING OUR WAKEFULNESS, WE SOMETIMES PRETEND NOTHING IS WRONG AS A
WAY OF COPING WITH A DIFFICULT CIRCUMSTANCE. DENYING FEELINGS IS LIKE A
BAND-AID: IT WORKS ON A SUPERFICIAL LEVEL, BUT THE DEEPER SCAR STILL HURTS
BENEATH. THE GRADUAL ACCUMULATION OF UNSOLVED EMOTIONAL SCARS CAN
AFFECT EVERYDAY LIFE AND INCREASE STRESS.

SOMETIMES GRIEF BREAKS THROUGH DURING DREAMS, AND YOU WAKE UP IN
TEARS, BECAUSE YOUR SUBCONSCIOUS IS HELPING YOU RELEASE FEELINGS
THAT ARE HARD TO PROCESS DURING THE DAY.

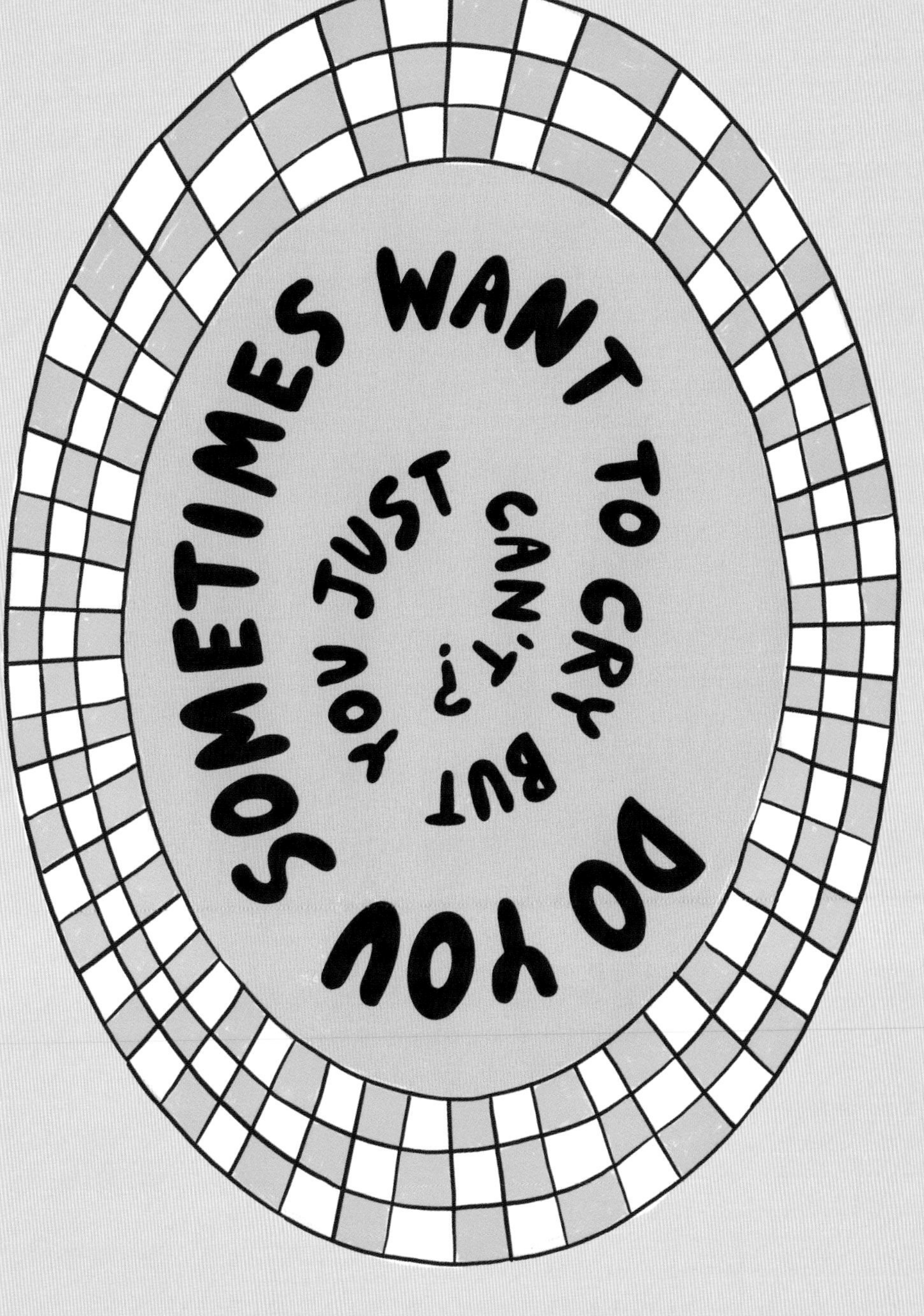
DO YOU SOMETIMES WANT TO CRY BUT YOU JUST CAN'T?

REASONS WHY YOU MIGHT NOT BE ABLE TO CRY

SOME PEOPLE FEEL THE SENSATION OF CRYING, THOUGH THEIR TEARS STILL WON'T FALL. OTHERS DON'T FEEL LIKE CRYING AT ALL.

PSYCHOLOGISTS HAVE DRAWN NEW THEORIES ABOUT PEOPLE WHO CAN'T PRODUCE TEARS—WHETHER EMOTIONAL TEARS OR THE BASAL TEARS THAT KEEP EYES MOISTURIZED. THERAPISTS HIGHLIGHT THE FACT THAT EMOTIONAL COMMUNICATION IS COMPROMISED IN THOSE WHO LACK TEARS.

A LACK OF TEARS CAN BE DUE TO A MEDICAL ISSUE TOO.
SOME MEDICAL EXPLANATIONS INCLUDE:

KERATOCONJUNCTIVITIS SICCA
"DRY EYE" INVOLVES A DECREASE IN TEAR PRODUCTION AND USUALLY IS ASSOCIATED WITH THE FOLLOWING:
* PREGNANCY OR MENOPAUSE-RELATED HORMONE CHANGES
* AGE, AS DRY EYES ARE FAIRLY COMMON IN OLDER ADULTHOOD
* DIABETES
* THYROID PROBLEMS
* RHEUMATOID ARTHRITIS
* CONTACT LENS USE
* EYELID INFLAMMATION OR DISORDERS

OTHER REASONS WHY YOU MIGHT NOT BE ABLE TO CRY

SJÖGREN'S SYNDROME:

THIS IS AN AUTOIMMUNE CONDITION THAT OFTEN DEVELOPS WITH A VIRAL OR BACTERIAL INFECTION. SJÖGREN'S SYNDROME CAUSES THE WHITE BLOOD CELLS IN YOUR BODY TO ATTACK THE GLANDS THAT PRODUCE MOISTURE, LIKE TEAR DUCTS AND MUCOUS MEMBRANES. THIS CAN CAUSE DRY EYES AND A DRY MOUTH.

MEDICATIONS

SOME MEDICATIONS CAN ALSO LEAD TO DECREASED TEAR PRODUCTION. YOU MIGHT NOTICE DIFFICULTY PRODUCING TEARS WHEN TAKING ANY OF THESE:
* BLOOD PRESSURE MEDICATIONS
* BIRTH CONTROL PILLS, ESPECIALLY IF YOU ALSO WEAR CONTACT LENSES
* SELECTIVE SEROTONIN REUPTAKE INHIBITORS
* ANTIHISTAMINES OR DECONGESTANTS

ENVIRONMENTAL FACTORS

A DRY OR WINDY CLIMATE MIGHT BE THE REASON YOU DON'T PRODUCE AS MANY TEARS. THIS HAPPENS BECAUSE THE DRYNESS OF THE AIR CAUSES TEARS TO EVAPORATE QUICKLY. THIS CAN ALSO OCCUR IF THE AIR BECOMES SMOKY DUE TO WILDFIRES OR OTHER EXTRAORDINARY ENVIRONMENTAL CAUSES.

PSYCHOLOGICAL FACTORS THAT CAN AFFECT YOUR CRYING

IN THE ABSENCE OF A MEDICAL CONDITION IMPACTING TEAR PRODUCTION, THE POSSIBLE REASON FOR YOUR REDUCED TEARS MIGHT BE CONNECTED TO EMOTIONAL OR PSYCHOLOGICAL ELEMENTS.

DIFFERENT SUBTYPES OF DEPRESSION CAN RESULT IN NUMEROUS SYMPTOMS, INCLUDING NOT PRODUCING TEARS. NOT ALL PEOPLE LIVING WITH DEPRESSION WILL NECESSARILY EXPERIENCE DEPRESSION IN THE EXACT SAME WAY.

MELANCHOLIC DEPRESSION

WITH THIS TYPE OF DEPRESSION, YOU MIGHT FEEL:
* UNEMOTIONAL OR "FLAT";
* SLOWED DOWN;
* HOPELESS, BLEAK, OR DESPAIRING; OR
* DISINTERESTED IN THE WORLD AROUND YOU

ANHEDONIA

ANHEDONIA DESCRIBES A LOSS OF INTEREST IN SOCIAL ACTIVITIES OR PHYSICAL SENSATIONS. YOU DON'T JUST EXPERIENCE A DECLINE IN PLEASURE; YOU MIGHT ALSO NOTICE A LOWER CAPACITY FOR EXPRESSING YOUR EMOTIONS. SOME PEOPLE WITH ANHEDONIA NOTICE THEY CAN NO LONGER CRY EASILY— OR AT ALL.

REPRESSED EMOTIONS

SOME INDIVIDUALS HAVE A HARD TIME MANAGING EMOTIONS, SO THEY PUSH THEM ASIDE OR HIDE THEM COMPLETELY IN ORDER TO COPE.
THIS SUPPRESSION MIGHT HAPPEN INTENTIONALLY AT FIRST BUT BECOME MORE AUTOMATIC OVER TIME.
IN TIME, YOU MIGHT EXPERIENCE MOST OF YOUR EMOTIONS MILDLY. EVEN IF SOMETHING DEEPLY SAD HAPPENS, YOU MIGHT NOT DISPLAY MUCH OF A REACTION.
REPRESSING EMOTIONS DOES NOT AFFECT YOUR PHYSICAL ABILITY TO CRY, BUT THE TEARS STILL WON'T COME.

PERSONAL FEELINGS ABOUT CRYING

IT'S TRUE THAT SOME PEOPLE MAY BELIEVE THAT CRYING EXPOSES VULNERABILITY OR SUGGESTS WEAKNESS, AND AS A RESULT, THEY MAY TRY TO SUPPRESS THEIR TEARS INTENTIONALLY. OVER TIME, WITH REPEATED EFFORTS TO HOLD BACK TEARS, SOME INDIVIDUALS MAY FIND THAT THEY BECOME LESS PRONE TO CRYING, AND THE TEARS MAY STOP COMING AS FREQUENTLY.

PEOPLE OFTEN START TO SEE CRYING AS A SIGN OF WEAKNESS WHEN THOSE AROUND THEM, INCLUDING PARENTS, SIBLINGS, AND PEERS, SHAME THEM FOR CRYING IN CHILDHOOD.

AN INABILITY TO CRY CAN ALSO REINFORCE A LEARNED BEHAVIOR. IF YOU NEVER SEE YOUR FAMILY MEMBERS AND LOVED ONES CRY, YOU MAY NEVER LEARN TO PERCEIVE CRYING AS A NATURAL FORM OF EMOTIONAL EXPRESSION.

DO YOU OFTEN HOLD BACK YOUR TEARS?

WHEN YOU ARE ON THE VERGE OF CRYING BUT TRY TO BLOCK YOUR TEARS, YOUR BRAIN REGISTERS TENSION AND STRESS. THE SYMPATHETIC NERVOUS SYSTEM SPEEDS UP YOUR HEART RATE AND INCREASES THE CONTRACTIONS OF YOUR HEART MUSCLE. THERE'S AN ALMOST ZEN-LIKE STATE THAT OCCURS AFTER CRYING, AND IT'S BECAUSE YOUR BREATHING STABILIZES, AND YOUR HEART RATE DECREASES.

SUNDAY, JANUARY 17TH, 2021. I CRIED FOR NOT HAVING CRIED.

THE BENEFITS OF A GOOD CRY

* IT HAS SELF-SOOTHING EFFECTS.

* IT'S A WAY OF ASKING FOR HELP AND GETTING SUPPORT FROM OTHERS.

* IT RELEASES STRESSORS AND TOXINS.

* IT HAS SLEEP-ENHANCING EFFECTS.

* IT KEEPS YOUR EYES CLEAN.

* IT MIGHT GIVE YOUR MOOD A BOOST.

* IT HELPS YOU RECOVER FROM GRIEF.

* IT RESTORES YOUR EMOTIONAL BALANCE.

* IT CAN BE A WAY OF EXPRESSING PROFOUND LOVE.

* IT CAN HELP YOU CONNECT WITH ART.

NOSTALGIA

HAVE YOU EVER SMELLED A PERFUME THAT TRANSPORTED YOU BACK TO YOUR CHILDHOOD AND SUDDENLY MADE YOU WANT TO CRY? NOSTALGIA IS A COMPLEX FEELING THAT CAN BE DESCRIBED AS BITTERSWEET. THIS EMOTION CAN BE TRIGGERED BY FAMILIAR SMELLS, OLD PHOTOS, HOMEMADE FOOD, OLD PLACES, OR PROBABLY ANYTHING THAT CAN BRING BACK A MEMORY.

I DON'T LIVE TRAPPED IN MY OWN MEMORIES, BUT I ENJOY ACTIVATING ROSY RECOLLECTIONS TO FEEL LOVE AND HOPE.
I USUALLY END UP CRYING WHEN I LOOK AT OLD FAMILY PHOTOS AND VIDEOS, BUT I TRY TO USE THOSE FEELINGS AND MEMORIES TO PROPEL ME INTO A BRILLIANT FUTURE.

 FRIDAY, APRIL 14TH, 2023. I CRIED IN THE HAIR SALON AFTER GETTING THE SAME HAIRCUT I HAD WHEN I WAS SIX YEARS OLD.

CRYING SKYMILES

I WAS TWENTY-THREE WHEN I FIRST MOVED TO A DIFFERENT CONTINENT BY MYSELF. I HAD WON A SCHOLARSHIP TO STUDY PHOTOGRAPHY AT THE ISTITUTO EUROPEO DI DESIGN IN MILAN, AND I RAPIDLY DECIDED TO LEAVE BEHIND MY SOUTH AMERICAN HOMETOWN AND MOVE TO THE ITALIAN CITY.

I STILL REMEMBER MY PARENTS' FACES WHEN THEY SAID GOODBYE TO ME AT THE AIRPORT— IT FELT LIKE THEY WERE ALSO SAYING GOODBYE TO MY WHOLE CHILDHOOD. I STARTED CRYING AS SOON AS I SAT IN MY DESIGNATED SEAT AND CONTINUED TO SHED TEARS FOR THE ENTIRE FLIGHT. I CRIED AS ONE CREW MEMBER ASKED ME IF I WANTED SOMETHING TO EAT. I SOBBED WATCHING *MAMMA MIA!* ON THE TINY AIRPLANE SCREEN.

PRACTICALLY EVERY AIR TRAVELER WANTS TO AVOID SITTING NEAR A CRYING BABY,
YET ADULTS ARE GUILTY OF BAWLING AND SOBBING IN-FLIGHT TOO.
THE WORLD HEALTH ORGANIZATION AFFIRMS THAT THE CHANGE IN AIR PRESSURE
INSIDE FLIGHT CABINS AND THE PERCEIVED LACK OF CONTROL OVER
THE ENVIRONMENT CAN AFFECT PEOPLE PHYSIOLOGICALLY, LEADING TO DEHYDRATION
AND EMOTIONAL BREAKDOWNS ONCE IN THE AIR.

FOR ANXIOUS PEOPLE LIKE ME, MERELY PLANNING A TRIP OR ARRIVING AT AN AIRPORT CAN
SIGNAL A THREAT TO THE BRAIN. THE STRESS LEADING TO THE JOURNEY CAN
RESULT IN THE EMOTIONAL RELEASE OF CRYING ONCE IN FLIGHT.
SAYING GOODBYE TO LOVED ONES WHO STAY BEHIND WHILE YOU TRAVEL, EVEN IF IT'S
ON VACATION, IS EMOTIONALLY MOVING.

PLANE CRYING STYLES

THE "HOLLYWOOD" CRIER: THEY WEAR DARK GLASSES AND A HAT ON EVERY FLIGHT. YOU MAY CONFUSE THEM WITH CELEBRITIES.

THE TISSUE MASTER: COVERS THE AIRPLANE TRAY TABLE WITH TISSUE BOXES. ALWAYS READY FOR A GOOD CRY IN THE SKY.

THE MYSTERIOUS PASSENGER: THEY HIDE UNDER THE BLANKETS AND GET OFF THE PLANE PRETENDING THEY HAD SOMETHING IN THEIR EYE.

THE WATERFALL ICON: THEY PICK THE SADDEST MOVIE ON THE IN-FLIGHT ENTERTAINMENT SCREEN AND OPEN THE TEAR DUCTS WITH NO SHAME.

THE HAPPY SOBBER: THEY ARE SO HAPPY TO GET TO THEIR FINAL DESTINATION THAT THEY CRY AND CLAP WHEN THE PLANE HITS THE TARMAC.

163

CRYING AND GRIEF

DEATH IS UBIQUITOUS, THE INEXORABLE END OF OUR HUMAN EXISTENCE. HOWEVER, CULTURAL RESPONSES TO GRIEF ARE NOT ALWAYS THE SAME. ALL SOCIETIES MANAGE THEIR GOODBYES IN DIFFERENT WAYS. ALTHOUGH CEREMONIES ARE SPECIFIC TO A GIVEN CULTURE AND LOCATION, THE TENDENCY TO CRY AT DEATH IS PRETTY COMMON ALL AROUND THE WORLD.

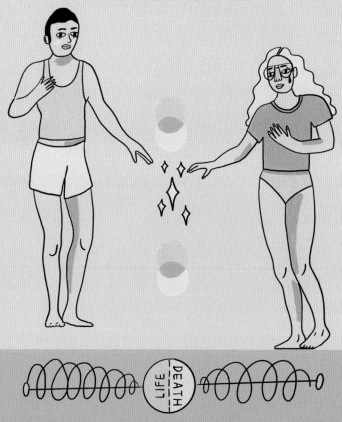

GRIEVING IS A LONG PROCESS. IT INVOLVES PERIODS OF ANGER, RAGE, SORROW, NUMBNESS, GUILT, AND STUPEFACTION. CRYING IS PARTICULARLY IMPORTANT, AS IT MAY HELP US PROCESS AND ACCEPT THE LOSS OF A LOVED ONE.

 WEDNESDAY, APRIL 6TH, 2022. I CRIED ALL DAY BECAUSE MY GRANDMOTHER ANGELA PASSED AWAY. I FELT DEHYDRATED AND DEFORMED.

COMING TO TERMS WITH THE LOSS OF A LOVED ONE IS NEVER AN EASY PROCESS, BUT TEARS USUALLY HELP US MOVE PAST THE HURT TO CELEBRATE THE LIFE AND PRECIOUS TIME WE SHARED WITH THEM.

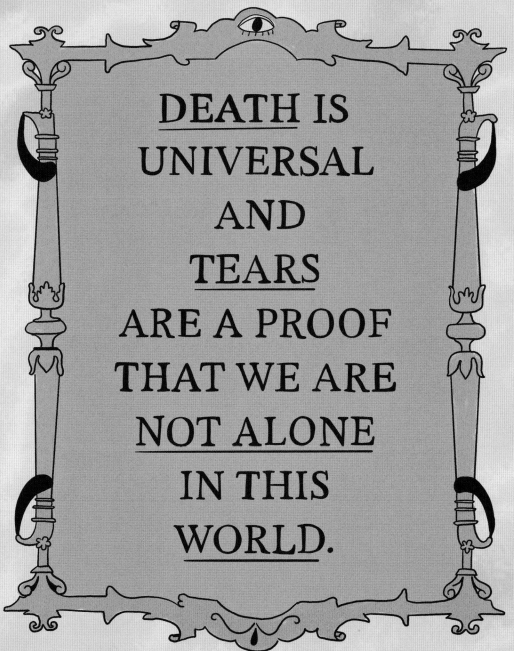

DEATH IS UNIVERSAL AND TEARS ARE A PROOF THAT WE ARE NOT ALONE IN THIS WORLD.

165

WHEN MY ADORED GRANDMOTHER ANGELA PASSED, I WAS 5,295 MILES AWAY FROM HER HOME. THAT DAY, MY DAD CALLED TO TELL ME HER HEART HAD FINALLY STOPPED. I STARTED CRYING AS I WALKED THE CROWDED STREETS OF NEW YORK CITY. WHEN I GOT HOME, I CRIED FOR FOUR STRAIGHT DAYS. WHENEVER I STOPPED SOBBING, I REMEMBERED SOMETHING ABOUT HER, THOUGHT OF ONE OF OUR ADVENTURES TOGETHER, AND STARTED CRYING AGAIN.

AFTER THE TEARS WASHED AWAY THE SADNESS INSIDE MY BRAIN, ONLY THE PUREST LOVE REMAINED. SIX MONTHS AFTER HER DEATH, I WENT BACK TO BUENOS AIRES AND VISITED HER HOUSE. I FOUND A PICTURE OF US AND A PEARL NECKLACE THAT I PUT ON AROUND MY NECK. THE TEARS PRESERVED THE MEMORIES OF OUR TIME TOGETHER, AND THE MEMORIES TURNED INTO SHINY TREASURES INSIDE MY MIND.

COLLECTIVE GRIEF

COLLECTIVE GRIEF HAPPENS WHEN A COMMUNITY, SOCIETY, OR NATION EXPERIENCES EXTREME CHANGE OR LOSS. COLLECTIVE GRIEF CAN MANIFEST DUE TO A MAJOR EVENT, SUCH AS A WAR, NATURAL DISASTER, PANDEMIC, OR OTHER EPISODE THAT RESULTS IN MASS CASUALTIES OR TRAGEDY.

WHEN GRIEF IS COLLABORATIVE, THE HEALING SHOULD BE AS WELL. WHEN A TRAGEDY OF ANY NATURE STRIKES A COMMUNITY, IT AFFECTS NOT ONLY EACH INDIVIDUAL IN THEIR OWN WAY BUT THE COMMUNITY AS A WHOLE. COMING TOGETHER TO MOURN AND GRIEVE PUBLICLY HELPS TO REAFFIRM THOSE SOCIAL BONDS. INSTEAD OF LEAVING EACH MEMBER OF THE COMMUNITY TO GRIEVE ON THEIR OWN, PUBLIC MOURNING AND GRIEVING CAN HELP KEEP EVERYONE CONNECTED AND STRONG.

THERE ARE THERAPEUTIC POWERS IN SOLIDARITY—JUST SEEING HOW THE COMMUNITY AROUND US UNITES IN EMOTIONAL RECOVERY CAN HELP US, AS INDIVIDUALS, HEAL FROM LOSS AND SORROW.

CRYING TOGETHER KEEPS US TOGETHER

 TUESDAY, FEBRUARY 8TH, 2022. I CRIED WHILE GOING THROUGH AIRPORT SECURITY. ANOTHER GIRL WAS ALSO CRYING NEXT TO ME. WE CRIED TOGETHER WITHOUT SAYING A WORD.

CRYING ROOMS

A CRYING ROOM IS A DESIGNATED AREA WHERE PEOPLE CAN BRING BABIES OR SMALL CHILDREN TO PREVENT THEIR OUTBURSTS FROM DISTRACTING OTHERS. THESE ROOMS BECAME POPULAR IN THE 1950S AND ARE USUALLY FOUND IN CHURCHES, THEATERS, AND CINEMAS. CRYING ROOMS ARE OFTEN DESIGNED WITH SOUNDPROOFING MATERIALS TO DECREASE THE NOISE.

IN 2021, LA LLORERÍA,
OR "THE CRYING ROOM," OPENED IN THE HEART OF MADRID.
IT WAS A PINK ROOM WHERE YOU COULD GO CRY.
THE PROJECT AIMED TO REMOVE THE STIGMA IN SOCIETY ATTACHED
TO MENTAL HEALTH, CRYING, AND SEEKING HELP. ANYONE WAS
ALLOWED TO VISIT. THE NAME ALLUDED TO THE POPULAR EXPRESSION "VE A
LLORAR A LA LLORERÍA" (GO CRY TO THE PLACE TO CRY).

CRYING AT WEDDINGS

EVERY NIGHT OF THE YEAR 1996, I ASKED MY MOM TO PUT ON MY PARENTS' WEDDING VHS. IN MY MIND IT WAS THE BEST MOVIE EVER MADE. I BECAME OBSESSED WITH THE '80S FOOD AND GOWNS, AND I WOULD CRY AT MY PARENTS DANCING THE WALTZ. I CRIED FOR A PART OF MY OWN HISTORY I WASN'T EVEN ALIVE FOR.

 FRIDAY, JUNE 3RD, 2022. I CRIED, AND THEN MADE THE SYMBOL OF "PEACE AND LOVE" WITH MY FINGERS.

TEARS ALLOW US TO CELEBRATE AND MOURN, TO EMBRACE NEW FEELINGS AND LET GO OF OLD, BURIED PAIN.

TEARS STAND FOR THE TENSION OF OPPOSITES. RIGHT UNDER HAPPY TEARS AND JOYFUL OCCASIONS, THERE IS A REMEMBERED LOSS FOR A TIME THAT IS GONE.

"MAY THE TRUE LOVE YOU SHARE ALLOW YOU TO ALWAYS CRY AND WALK TOGETHER."

PARTNERS IN CRYING

IN EVERY HUMAN RELATIONSHIP, WHENEVER YOU CRY WITH SOMEONE AND YOU SHARE BLISS OR SORROW, YOU BECOME ONE. BY UNITING IN GENUINE TEARS, YOU EXPAND LOVE AND PEACE IN THE WORLD. CANDID CRYING AND TRUE LOVE ENLARGE US AND GIVE US SPACE TO BE GOOD-HEARTED.

CRYING TOGETHER FOREVER.

 SUNDAY, JANUARY 9TH, 2022. I CRIED WITH MY PARTNER, WHILE HE WAS GIVING ME A HORMONAL INJECTION.

GIVING SOMEONE CRYING VALIDATION IS ESSENTIALLY TELLING THEM THAT THEIR REACTION MAKES SENSE AND THAT THEY CAN EXPRESS EMOTION IN A PHYSICAL WAY.
HUMANS ARE VERY DIVERSE AND REACT IN DIFFERENT WAYS, SO ACKNOWLEDGING OTHER PEOPLE'S TEARS AND FEELINGS AS VALID IS VERY HEALING FOR EVERYONE, AND IS GOOD PRACTICE FOR CHILDREN AND ADULTS.

INTIMATE CRYING

CRYING DURING CONSENSUAL SEX CAN BE A COMPLETELY NORMAL EXPERIENCE. AN INTENSE ORGASM LIGHTS UP THE WHOLE BRAIN AND ALL EMOTIONS ARE AMPLIFIED. THE COMBINATION OF PHYSICAL AND EMOTIONAL INTENSITY CAN MAKE YOU TEAR UP OR CRY FROM THE EXTRAORDINARY PLEASURE.

THESE MIGHT BE HAPPY TEARS, TEARS OF RELIEF, OR A BIT OF MELANCHOLY. TEARS DURING OR AFTER SEX CAN ALSO BE A PURE PHYSICAL REACTION.

WHAT TO DO ABOUT CRYING DURING SEXUAL INTERCOURSE

FOR PHYSICAL PAIN OR DISCOMFORT DURING OR AFTER SEX, SEE A MEDICAL PROFESSIONAL. MANY FACTORS THAT CAUSE THIS TYPE OF SUFFERING ARE TREATABLE.

OTHERWISE, QUESTION AND REFLECT ON THE REASONS BEHIND YOUR CRYING:

- DID YOUR TEARS FEEL PHYSICAL OR EMOTIONAL?

- WAS IT JUST A FEW REFLEX TEARS OR WERE YOU TRULY CRYING?

- WHAT WAS GOING THROUGH YOUR MIND WHEN THE CRYING STARTED? WERE YOUR THOUGHTS PLEASANT OR DISTURBING?

- DID TEARS RELIEVE YOUR TENSION OR ADD TO IT?

WHAT TO DO IF YOUR SEXUAL PARTNER CRIES:

- ASK IF SOMETHING IS WRONG, BUT TRY NOT TO CRITICIZE. TALK TO THEM GENTLY.

- OFFER COMFORT, BUT RESPECT THEM IF THEY NEED SOME SPACE.

- ASK HOW YOU CAN HELP.

- GIVE THEM TIME. BRING IT UP LATER. DON'T FORCE THE ISSUE IF THEY STILL DON'T WANT TO DISCUSS IT.

- JUST BE THERE FOR THEM.

IF THE PROCESS OF UNDERSTANDING TEARS DURING SEX BRINGS UP PAINFUL MEMORIES OR UNPLEASANT EMOTIONS, IT'S ESSENTIAL NOT TO REGARD CRYING AS INSIGNIFICANT.

 FRIDAY, FEBRUARY 18TH, 2022. I CRIED WHILE OPENING UP TO MY PARTNER, AND ALL THE WORDS CAME OUT BROKEN.

TO ME, SOMETIMES TEARS CAN FEEL CONTAGIOUS. I FIND THAT PEOPLE WHO DETACH THEMSELVES WHEN I CRY IN FRONT OF THEM, OR ASK ME TO STOP CRYING, ARE LESS COMFORTABLE WITH THEIR OWN PERSONAL EMOTIONS AND DON'T WANT TO START CRYING BY EMOTIONAL TRANSFERENCE. MAYBE OTHERS FEEL LIKE MY TEARS WILL FORCE THEM TO FACE FEELINGS THEY ARE NOT READY TO FACE, AND THAT'S OKAY.

WHENEVER I'M CRYING OUT OF HAPPINESS OR SADNESS, I WISH MORE PEOPLE WOULD SOB ALONG WITH ME TO CREATE A CRYING SYMPHONY.

 THURSDAY, FEBRUARY 10TH, 2022. I CRIED WATCHING AN ICE-SKATING PERFORMANCE AT THE WINTER OLYMPICS ON TV. MY TEARS FELT LIKE PART OF A SNOWFLAKE DANCE.

I USUALLY LIKE MY FACE AFTER A LITTLE CRY.

WHENEVER I FEEL TIRED OR UGLY, I BRING BACK SOME MENTAL MEMORIES TO MAKE MYSELF CRY A LITTLE. LATELY, I'VE BEEN THINKING ABOUT MY LATE GRANDMOTHER AND IT WORKS LIKE A CHARM.

I SHED A FEW TEARS ON THE TRAIN, BEFORE A MEETING OR ON MY WAY TO A DINNER PARTY.

CRY STREET

AFTER CRYING, I FEEL RESTED, SHINY, AND AS SOFT AS A FRESH CLOUD.

TEARS IN SPACE

IN SPACE, TEARS DON'T FALL DOWN BECAUSE OF ZERO GRAVITY.
INSTEAD, TEARS IN SPACE FORM A BALL AROUND THE EYES.
CLAYTON C. ANDERSON, A NASA ASTRONAUT, SAID THIS ABOUT HIS EXPERIENCE: "I CRIED IN SPACE SEVERAL TIMES...DUE TO SOME VERY EMOTIONAL CIRCUMSTANCES...CRYING IS EXACTLY THE SAME AS HERE ON EARTH, EXCEPT THE TEARS DON'T FALL DOWN...NOT A BIG DEAL AT ALL...THE EMOTIONS I EXPERIENCED, HOWEVER, WERE A BIG DEAL."

WEDNESDAY, OCTOBER 14TH, 2020. I CRIED LOOKING AT THE NIGHT SKY THROUGH THE WINDOW OF A MOVING CAR.

OUR PLANET IS SPECIAL. TEARS FALL DOWN ON EARTH.
EMOTIONAL WATERS FLOW DOWN OUR FACE, OVER
OUR CHEEKS, AND INTO OUR HEARTS,
LIKE A RIVER OF LOVE.

THERE IS NO SHAME IN CRYING ON PLANET EARTH.

CRYING OUT IN THE WORLD IS A RADICAL ACT.

CRYING IN THE SHOWER

PEOPLE WHO STRUGGLE TO FORM EMOTIONAL CONNECTIONS MAY FIND THEMSELVES MORE INCLINED TO TEAR UP IN THE SHOWER, AS IT OFFERS THEM PRIVACY, PREVENTING OTHERS FROM PERCEIVING THEM AS VULNERABLE. CRYING IN THE SHOWER COMBINES TWO COMFORTING HUMAN ACTIVITIES: WEEPING AND CLEANSING— IT CAN BE VERY CATHARTIC AND SATISFYING. I CRY AND GET MOST OF MY CREATIVE VISUALIZATION AND PROBLEM-SOLVING DONE WHILE I SHOWER.

 MONDAY, AUGUST 31ST, 2020. I CRIED AND DRANK WATER AT THE SAME TIME, DEHYDRATION AND HYDRATION.

HUMAN-ROBOT INTERACTION

MACHINES AND ARTIFICIAL INTELLIGENCE WOULDN'T EXIST WITHOUT HUMAN INTELLIGENCE. IT DOESN'T MATTER HOW WELL PEOPLE PROGRAM ROBOTS AND MACHINES; THE CAPACITY TO FEEL SPONTANEOUS EMOTION AND INTUITIVE EMPATHY IS WHAT MAKES OUR INTERACTIONS UNIQUELY AND INTRINSICALLY HUMAN.

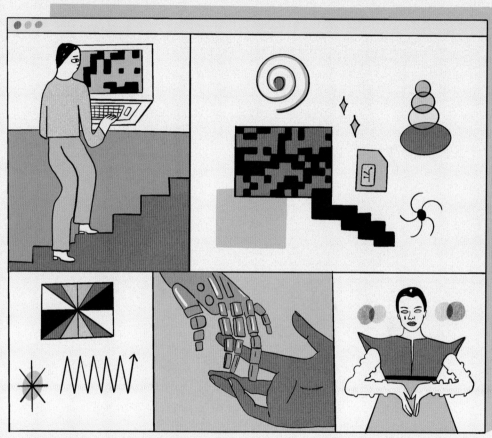

AS ARTIFICIAL INTELLIGENCE CHANGES AND EVOLVES, MORE TECH COMPANIES ARE EXPANDING TOOLS TO MEASURE EMOTIONS FROM VERBAL, FACIAL, AND VOCAL EXPRESSIONS. RESEARCHERS ARE RELEASING ADVANCED CHATBOTS THAT CAN CLOSELY MIMIC HUMAN EMOTIONS TO CREATE MORE-EMPATHETIC CONNECTIONS WITH USERS. THE PROBLEM IS THAT, EVEN THOUGH ALGORITHMS CAN PRODUCE IMAGES THAT MAKE US CRY, OR MIGHT BE TRAINED TO RECOGNIZE EXPRESSIONS OF EMOTION, THEY DON'T CONSIDER THE WHOLE SOCIAL CONTEXT OF THE SITUATION.
WHILE SOME SOFTWARE CAN RECOGNIZE THAT A PERSON IS CRYING, IT IS NOT POSSIBLE TO EXPLORE THE REASON AND MEANING BEHIND THE TEARS IN THAT EXACT MOMENT.

CRYING MAPS

CRYING MAPS OFFER PEOPLE A GUIDE TO THE BEST PLACES TO ENJOY
AND CELEBRATE A GOOD CRY.
"CRYING IN PUBLIC" IS A COLLABORATIVE MAPPING TOOL BUILT BY THE PROGRAMMER
KATE RAY. THE SITE PRESENTS VISITORS WITH A MAP OF THE NEW YORK CITY AREA
AND INVITES ANYONE TO MARK WITH AN EMOJI SITES WHERE THEY'VE WEPT
OR OTHERWISE FELT STRONG FEELINGS.

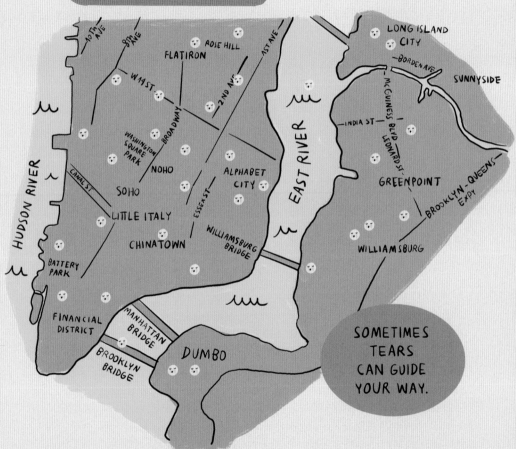

FOLLOW THE STEPS OF YOUR TEARS. HAVING A CRYING MAP FOR YOURSELF CAN
PROVIDE A GLIMPSE INTO THE MANY THINGS THAT MOVE YOU AND CAN ALSO
BECOME A DOCUMENT OF TIME, TO REGISTER AND REVISIT THINGS YOU'VE FELT
AND EXPERIENCES YOU'VE HAD.

YOUR OWN CRYING MAP

THINK OF ALL THE PUBLIC SPACES THAT GIVE YOU COMFORT. A SPECIFIC TREE IN THE PARK, YOUR LOCAL COFFEE SHOP, THE PLANETARIUM, THE OUTDOOR STAIRS AT THE PUBLIC LIBRARY, THE MAKEUP AISLE AT A DEPARTMENT STORE. GRAB OR PRINT A MAP OF YOUR CITY OR TOWN AND ADD ALL THE SPACES WHERE YOU FEEL SAFE. WHENEVER YOU FEEL LIKE CRYING OUTSIDE, GO TO YOUR CLOSEST SAFE CRYING SPOT. LET THE WAVES COME.

 WEDNESDAY, APRIL 14TH, 2021. I CRIED BECAUSE I WAS HOME.

Flower Brain

HEY! THERE ARE FLOWERS IN THE GARDEN OF YOUR MIND.

YOU HAVE PLANTED YOUR OWN MEMORIES.

YOU CAN SMELL YOUR THOUGHTS.

EAT THE VELVETY PETALS OF YOUR IDEAS

AND WATER YOUR BRAIN WITH TEARS UNTIL IT BLOOMS.

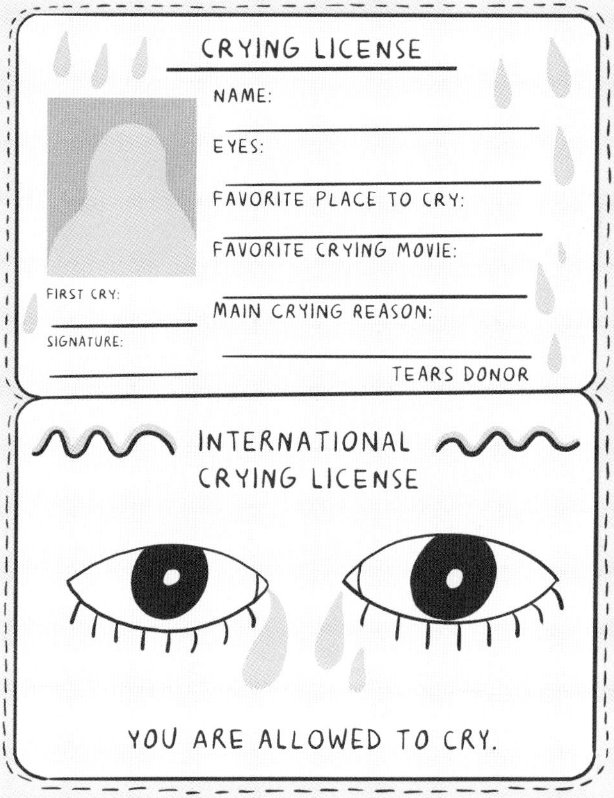
CRYING LICENSE
NAME:
EYES:
FAVORITE PLACE TO CRY:
FAVORITE CRYING MOVIE:
MAIN CRYING REASON:
FIRST CRY:
SIGNATURE:
TEARS DONOR
INTERNATIONAL CRYING LICENSE
YOU ARE ALLOWED TO CRY.

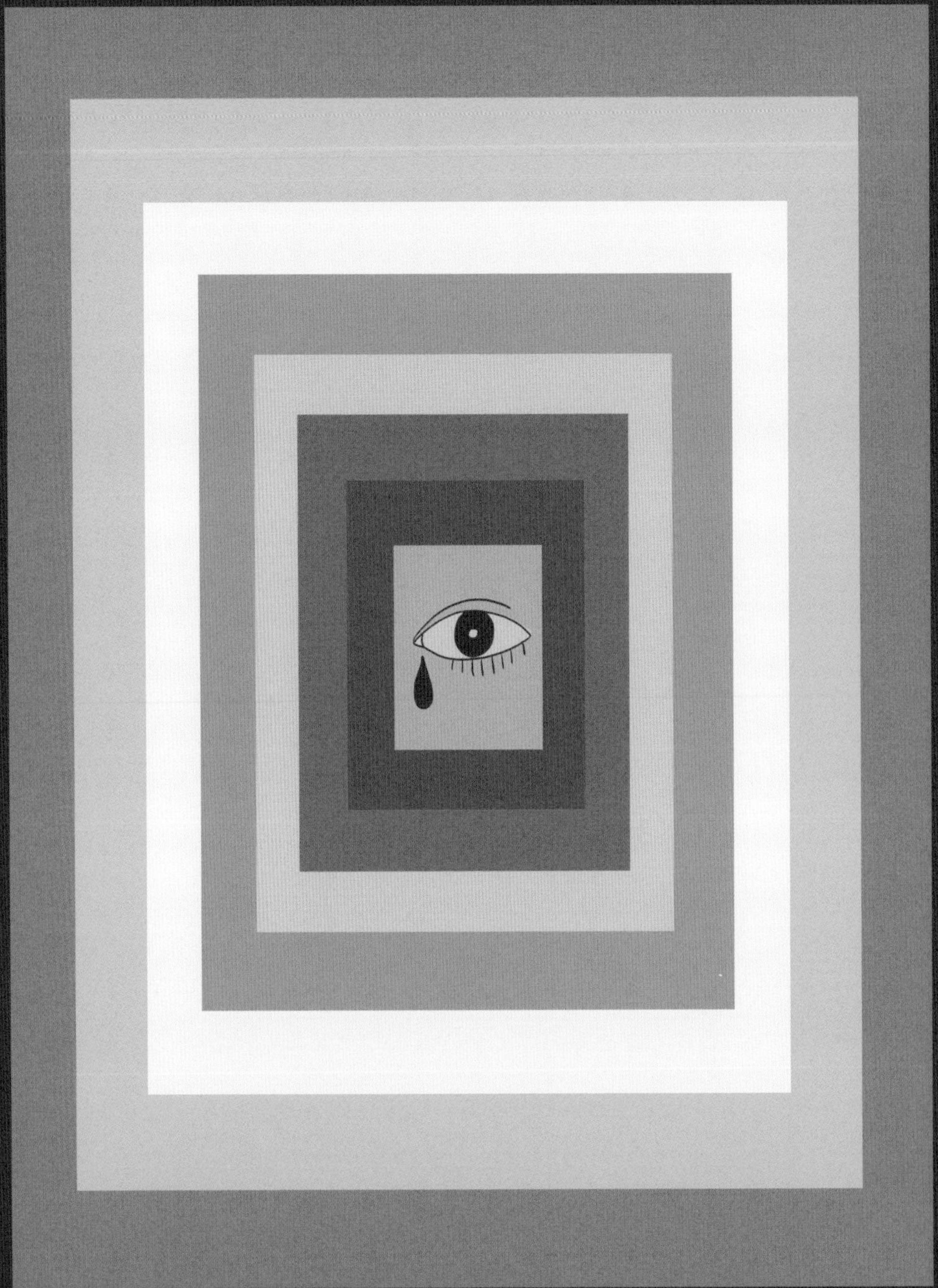

IN ORDER TO BENEFIT FROM CRYING AND FEEL THE POSITIVE IMPACT OF A POWERFUL CRY, IT'S IMPORTANT TO BE IN GOOD EMOTIONAL SHAPE. SOME WAYS TO IMPROVE AND REFINE COPING SYSTEMS AND EMOTIONAL SELF HEALTH:

NOTICE YOUR EMOTIONS AND REACTIONS. WHICH THINGS MAKE YOU SAD, FRUSTRATED, OR ANGRY?

EXPRESS YOUR FEELINGS. TELL PEOPLE CLOSE TO YOU WHEN SOMETHING IS BOTHERING YOU.

TAKE YOUR TIME. THINK AND BE CALM BEFORE YOU SAY OR DO SOMETHING YOU MIGHT REGRET.

LEAN INTO RELAXATION. TRY DEEP BREATHING, SOUND BATHS, MEDITATION, AND EXERCISE.

DO WHAT YOU CAN TO MAINTAIN A HEALTHY WORK-LIFE BALANCE.

FOCUS ON THE HAPPY MOMENTS IN YOUR LIFE.

TAKE CARE OF YOUR PHYSICAL HEALTH, EXERCISE, AND EAT HEALTHY.

STAY IN TOUCH AND CONNECT WITH PEOPLE WHO HAVE A POSITIVE IMPACT IN YOUR LIFE.

POST–GOOD CRY

AFTER A GOOD CRYING SPELL, YOU CAN BE MORE HOPEFUL ABOUT THE FUTURE AHEAD.

SOME THINGS YOU MIGHT ENJOY DURING OR AFTER CRYING:

- WASHING YOUR FACE

- TAKING A FEW DEEP BREATHS

- JOURNALING AND WRITING DOWN YOUR THOUGHTS

- TAKING A SHOWER

- TAKING A NAP

- DRINKING WATER OR TEA

- GOING FOR A WALK

- TALKING TO A FRIEND OR SOMEONE YOU LOVE

- CRYING AGAIN

THE ATTITUDE TOWARD THE EXPRESSION OR SUPPRESSION OF TEARS VARIES DEPENDING ON EACH SOCIETY AND CULTURE. THERE ARE CERTAIN TRIBES THAT USE CRYING AS A GREETING RITUAL INSTEAD OF KISSING, WAVING, OR SHAKING HANDS; THESE WEEPING RITUALS CAN STIMULATE FEELINGS OF UNITY DURING TIMES OF DEEP CRISIS WITHIN A COMMUNITY OR SOCIAL CONFLICT.

WE ARE ALL CONNECTED BY TEARS.

WHEN OTHERS IGNORE OR CRITICIZE SOMEONE WHO IS CRYING, IT BECOMES DIFFICULT FOR THE CRYING PERSON TO EXPERIENCE AN IMPROVEMENT IN THEIR MOOD. WHENEVER POSSIBLE, PEOPLE PREFER TO CRY IN THE PRESENCE OF SOMEONE WHO WILL GIVE THEM COMFORT AND SUPPORT, LIKE THEIR PARENTS, THEIR SIBLINGS, OR THEIR PARTNER. FOR CHILDREN, TEARS SERVE AS AN IMPORTANT COMMUNICATION TOOL, ALLOWING THEM TO SHOW THEIR EMOTIONAL NEEDS. THIS TOOL MAY ALSO BE POWERFUL IN ADULTHOOD. IGNORING SOMEONE WHO IS OPENLY CRYING IN PUBLIC IS ALMOST IMPOSSIBLE; OFTEN, A SORT OF EMPATHY ARISES WITHIN US WHEN FACED WITH SOMEONE'S TEARS. ACTUALLY, WHEN PUBLIC CRIERS DISCLOSE THAT THEY WERE HELPED AND SUPPORTED, THEY ALSO TEND TO REPORT FEELING BETTER AFTER CRYING THAN THOSE WHO WERE IGNORED.

THE POWER OF EMPATHY

UNDERSTANDING ANOTHER HUMAN'S SUFFERING OR HAPPINESS IS THE SWEETEST GIFT YOU CAN GIVE THEM. COMPASSION IS LOVE, AND FEELING WHAT OTHERS ARE FEELING IS LOVE MULTIPLIED.

CRYING HAPPENS ON OUR FACES, FOR ANYONE TO SEE. THE FACT THAT WE DON'T CRY OUT OF OUR ARMPITS SUGGESTS THAT HUMAN TEARS ARE A SOCIAL MECHANISM, AND THAT THERE'S AN EVOLUTIONARY ADVANTAGE TO LETTING OTHERS KNOW THAT WE'RE EXPERIENCING SOMETHING.

A TEAR IS A UNIVERSAL SIGN, AND CRYING IS EVOLUTION.
WHY IS IT NORMAL TO LAUGH TOGETHER AND CRY ALONE?

CRYING BRINGS OUT STRONG SOCIAL BONDING REACTIONS, AND PEOPLE
FEEL MUCH MORE INCLINED TO HELP THOSE WHO ARE VISIBLY PRODUCING TEARS.

UNDERSTANDING CRYING BRINGS COMPASSION AND RELIEF.

YOU CAN TRANSFORM YOUR OWN FEELINGS

AND HELP OTHERS BY LOOKING DEEPLY

INTO THEIR CRYING.

 SUNDAY, OCTOBER 24TH, 2021. I CRIED LOOKING FOR FILES ON AN EXTERNAL HARD DRIVE AND THOUGHT ABOUT THE PEOPLE WHO STORE MEMORIES FROM MY LIFE.

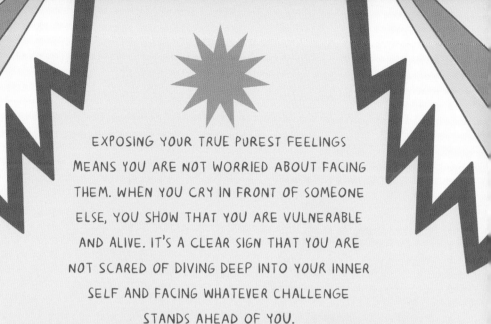

EXPOSING YOUR TRUE PUREST FEELINGS
MEANS YOU ARE NOT WORRIED ABOUT FACING
THEM. WHEN YOU CRY IN FRONT OF SOMEONE
ELSE, YOU SHOW THAT YOU ARE VULNERABLE
AND ALIVE. IT'S A CLEAR SIGN THAT YOU ARE
NOT SCARED OF DIVING DEEP INTO YOUR INNER
SELF AND FACING WHATEVER CHALLENGE
STANDS AHEAD OF YOU.

YOU HAVE NOTHING TO HIDE.

CRYING IS GOING TO HELP YOU
CONQUER THE UNKNOWN.

TEARS ARE A RELIEF VALVE, LARGELY BECAUSE KEEPING DIFFICULT AND OVERWHELMING FEELINGS INSIDE—WHAT PSYCHOLOGISTS CALL REPRESSIVE COPING—CAN BE BAD FOR OUR OVERALL HEALTH.
CRYING, AND OTHER FORMS OF EMOTIONAL RELEASE, ARE IMPORTANT PSYCHOLOGICAL TOOLS FOR OUR MINDS AND BODIES.

WEDNESDAY, APRIL 28TH, 2021. I CRIED LOOKING AT THE MENU IN AN ITALIAN RESTAURANT.

"KAMA MUTA" IS A SANSKRIT EXPRESSION USED TO DESCRIBE BEING "MOVED BY LOVE." THIS FEELING IS OFTEN TRIGGERED BY OBSERVING OR ENGAGING IN SOMEONE ELSE'S EMOTION, AND WE SUDDENLY FEEL A STRONG CONNECTION AND A SENSE OF ONENESS. PEOPLE WITH HIGH EMPATHY ARE PARTICULARLY LIKELY TO CRY IN RESPONSE TO OTHER PEOPLE'S TEARS. BEING MOVED BY OTHER PEOPLE'S TEARS IS A POWERFUL KIND OF CRY.

THE UNIVERSE IS WITHIN YOU,

BUT YOU ARE NOT THE CENTER OF THE UNIVERSE.

YOU ARE FLOATING AMONG

BILLIONS OF STARS.

 WEDNESDAY, OCTOBER 6TH, 2021. I CRIED BECAUSE CRYING IS TRENDING AND WE ALL SHOULD SHED TEARS TOGETHER TO MAKE A BETTER WORLD.

THERE'S A MAGICAL PLACE

WHERE TEARS MEET LAUGHTER

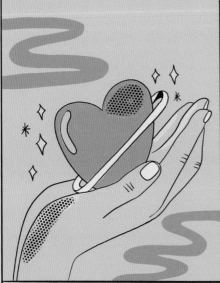

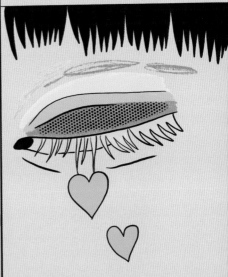

AND IT FEELS LIKE THE
ULTIMATE HUMAN EXPERIENCE.

CAN YOU
IMAGINE
THE TEARS
OF THE
FUTURE?

THANK YOU

I WANT TO THANK EVERYONE WHO HAS CRIED WITH ME THROUGHOUT THE LONG, THREE-YEAR PROCESS OF MAKING THIS BOOK—A LABOR OF LOVE, SWEAT, AND TEARS.

I'D ALSO LIKE TO THANK ANYONE—FRIEND OR STRANGER—WHO HAS CRIED WITH ME THROUGHOUT LIFE IN GENERAL.

I ESPECIALLY WANT TO THANK GUIDO, MY PARTNER IN CRYING AND IN LIFE. WITHOUT HIS SUPPORT AND EMPATHY, I COULDN'T HAVE FINISHED THIS PROJECT. HE HAS SEEN ME CRY MORE THAN ANY OTHER HUMAN BEING AND HAS ALWAYS BEEN READY TO SUPPORT ME WITH HUGS AND TISSUES.

I'D ALSO LIKE TO THANK MY PARENTS, WHO WELCOMED ME INTO THIS WORLD CRYING AND HAVE TEARED UP WHENEVER I ACHIEVED MAJOR MILESTONES. THEIR TEARS HAVE ALWAYS MADE ME FEEL LOVED AND SUPPORTED. MY MOM, WHO WAS THE FIRST TO EVER RESPOND TO MY CRYING—SHE'S MY BIGGEST CHEERLEADER AND TEAR LEADER. MY DAD, FOR ALWAYS WRITING LETTERS THAT MAKE ME CRY OUT LOUD. MY BROTHERS, FOR BEING THE KEEPERS OF THE SENSITIVE DATA FROM OUR CHILDHOOD. MY NEPHEWS, BATU AND ALFONSO, FOR MAKING MY HEART BURST INTO TEARS OF EVER-EXPANDING LOVE.

I'D LIKE TO THANK ALL OF MY FRIENDS; WITHOUT THEM, LIFE AND TEARS MAKE NO SENSE. ROSARIO, FOR KNOWING ME SO WELL. LULES, FOR HER EXTRAORDINARY EMPATHY TOWARD ALL LIVING THINGS. IAIR, FOR ALWAYS ANSWERING MY CALLS. ANGIE, FOR TAKING CARE OF EVERYONE. LULA, FOR ALWAYS HAVING ENLIGHTENED ADVICE. ANA, FOR WALKING WITH ME. MALÉN, FOR ALWAYS INSPIRING ME WITH HER POETRY. MELINA, FOR HER LAUGHTER AND HUMOR. LU, FOR HER SPECIAL SENSITIVITY. ANTO, MARTIN, AND RIO, FOR THEIR CLOSENESS. CARLOS, FOR HIS INFINITE KINDNESS. SEBAS, FOR OUR TELEPATHIC FRIENDSHIP. COCO, FOR SHARING THE PROCESS. ALL MY FRIENDS AT THE CENTER FOR CARTOON STUDIES. MY KIND SUPPORTERS AT THE CRYING CLUB: LUISINA, ANNA, AUTUMN, LISA, JANEL, EU, DAN, INÉS, AND ELLYNNE. AND AD VINGERHOETS, FOR DOING AN EXTENSIVE JOB IN THE RESEARCH OF HUMAN TEARS.

TO EUGENIA, FOR INTRODUCING ME TO MY BRIGHT AGENT, DANIELLE, WHOM I'M ALSO VERY GRATEFUL FOR.

TO MY WONDERFUL EDITORS, EMMA, HELENA, THEA, AND MICHAEL, FOR LEADING THE WAY WITH THEIR KIND WORDS AND THOUGHTFUL SUGGESTIONS.

TO EVERYONE WHO WILL CRY WITH ME IN THE FUTURE.

IF YOU FEEL EXTREMELY SAD AND ARE THINKING ABOUT SUICIDE, ARE WORRIED ABOUT A FRIEND OR LOVED ONE, OR WOULD LIKE EMOTIONAL SUPPORT, THE LIFELINE NETWORK IS AVAILABLE 24/7 ACROSS THE UNITED STATES. CALL 988. FOR GLOBAL READERS, FIND YOUR LOCAL HELPLINE AT: HTTPS://FINDAHELPLINE.COM.

SOURCES

CRYING: THE NATURAL AND CULTURAL HISTORY OF TEARS BY TOM LUTZ

"WHY DO WE CRY? THE SCIENCE OF TEARS" BY NICK KNIGHT

   https://www.independent.co.uk/life-style/why-do-we-cry-the-science-of-tears-9741287.html

"THE SCIENCE OF CRYING" BY MANDY OAKLANDER

   https://time.com/4254089/science-crying/

"ALL ABOUT EMOTIONAL TEARS" BY REENA MUKAMAL, AMERICAN ACADEMY OF OPHTHALMOLOGY

   https://www.aao.org/eye-health/tips-prevention/all-about-emotional-tears

"WHY WE CRY" BY CLEVELAND CLINIC

   https://health.clevelandclinic.org/tears-why-we-cry-and-more-infographic/#:~:text=3.%20Psychic%20or%20emotional%20tears

"DEAR SCIENCE: WHY DO WE CRY" BY SARAH KAPLAN

   https://www.washingtonpost.com/news/speaking-of-science/wp/2016/11/28/dear-science-why-do-we-cry/

"TEARS TEACHER: XWHEN WAS THE LAST TIME YOU CRIED?" BY NOEMIE NAKAI

   https://www.youtube.com/watch?v=CawT_sqi8xo

"WHY DO BABIES CRY ON AIRPLANES?" BY JANE LABOUS

   https://www.livescience.com/64714-why-babies-cry-on-airplanes.html

"A CRY FOR HELP" BY IAN MURSELL/MEXICOLORE

   https://www.mexicolore.co.uk/aztecs/aztec-life/cry-for-help

"TEARS AND CRYING IN GRAECO-ROMAN ANTIQUITY: AN INTRODUCTION" BY THORSTEN FOGEN

   https://www.degruyter.com/document/doi/10.1515/9783110214024.1/html

"CATHARSIS IN PSYCHOLOGY" BY KENDRA CHERRY

   https://www.verywellmind.com/what-is-catharsis-2794968#:~:text=a%20catharsis%20is%20an%20emotional,feelings%20of%20frustration%20and

   %20tension

"HISTORY OF LOVE HIDDEN IN LACHRYMATORY BOTTLES" BY ANADOLU AGENCY

   https://www.dailysabah.com/life/2020/02/14/history-of-love-hidden-in-lachrymatory-bottles

CRYING IN THE MIDDLE AGES: TEARS OF HISTORY BY ELINA GERTSMAN

"WHY WE CRY AT MOVIES" BY PAUL J. ZAK

   https://www.psychologytoday.com/us/blog/the-moral-molecule/200902/why-we-cry-movies

"TWO TYPES OF PEAK EMOTIONAL RESPONSES TO MUSIC: THE PSYCHOPHYSIOLOGY OF CHILLS AND TEARS" BY K. MORI AND M. IWANAGA

   https://www.nature.com/articles/srep46063

"MOVED TO TEARS" BY FRANCIS WILSON

   https://interlude.hk/moved-tears/

"CRYING WHILE READING THROUGH THE CENTURIES" BY PELAGIA HORGAN

   https://www.newyorker.com/books/page-turner/crying-while-reading-through-the-centuries

"LEADERS ARE CRYING ON THE JOB. MAYBE THAT'S A GOOD THING" BY JESSICA BENNETT

   https://www.nytimes.com/2020/05/03/us/politics/crying-politicians-leadership.html

CRYING AT THE MUSEUM: A CALL FOR RESPONSIBLE EMOTIONAL DESIGN [EXHIBITION] BY STACEY MANN

"THIS ART EXHIBITION IS GUARANTEED TO MAKE YOU WEEP" BY JASON DALEY

   https://www.smithsonianmag.com/smart-news/im-totally-not-crying-new-art-exhibit-guaranteed-make-you-weep-180970450/

"IS IT NORMAL TO CRY MORE DURING YOUR PERIOD?" BY COREY WHELAN

   https://www.healthline.com/health/womens-health/crying-during-period

"THIS IS WHAT HAPPENS TO YOUR BODY WHEN YOU CRY" BY MARYGRACE TAYLOR

   https://www.self.com/story/what-happens-when-you-cry

WHY ONLY HUMANS WEEP: UNRAVELLING THE MYSTERIES OF TEARS BY AD VINGERHOETS

"FILM CLUB: 'TEARS TEACHER'" BY THE LEARNING NETWORK

https://www.nytimes.com/2020/10/01/learning/film-club-tears-teacher.html

"THE RELATIONSHIP OF GENDER ROLES AND BELIEFS TO CRYING IN AN INTERNATIONAL SAMPLE" BY L. S. SHARMAN ET AL.

https://www.ncbi.nlm.nih.gov/pmc/articles/PMC6795704/

"THE LUXUTY OF TEARS" BY MATTHEW SWEET

https://www.economist.com/1843/2016/03/02/the-luxury-of-tears

"WHY IT'S OKAY TO CRY WITH PATIENTS AND THEIR FAMILIES" BY KATELYNNE SHEPARD

https://www.travelnursing.com/news/features-and-profiles/why-its-okay-to-cry-with-patients-and-their-families/

"CAN'T CRY? HERE'S WHAT MIGHT BE GOING ON" BY CRYSTAL RAYPOLE

https://www.healthline.com/health/mental-health/why-cant-i-cry

"THIS IS WHY YOU'RE MORE LIKELY TO CRY ON AN AIRPLANE, ACCORDING TO A PSYCHOLOGIST" BY MAHITA GAJANAN

https://time.com/5274209/airplane-cry-emotion/

"10 REASONS WHY CRYING DURING OR AFTER SEX IS COMPLETELY NORMAL" BY ANN PIETRANGELO

https://www.healthline.com/health/healthy-sex/crying-after-sex

"HERE'S HOW (AND WHY) TO HELP BOYS FEEL ALL THE FEELS" BY LENA ABURDENE DERHALLY

https://www.washingtonpost.com/news/parenting/wp/2015/10/01/boys-have-feelings-too-heres-how-to-help-them-feel-all-the-feels/

"STUDY REVEALS 5 MAIN REASONS THAT MAKE PEOPLE CRY" BY DEUTSCHE PRESSE-AGENTUR

https://www.dailysabah.com/life/study-reveals-5-main-reasons-that-make-people-cry/news

"WHY CRYING IS A FEMINIST ACT" BY OLIVIA COMSTOCK

https://uiwomenscenter.wordpress.com/2017/04/08/why-crying-is-a-feminist-act/

"LET THE TEARS FLOW: CRYING IS THE ULTIMATE HEALER" BY BOB LIVINGSTONE

https://www.mentalhelp.net/blogs/let-the-tears-flow-crying-is-the-ultimate-healer/

"9 WAYS CRYING MAY BENEFIT YOUR HEALTH" BY ASHLEY MARCIN

https://www.healthline.com/health/benefits-of-crying

"WHY DO WE LIKE SAD STORIES?" BY CYNTHIA VINNEY

https://www.verywellmind.com/why-do-we-like-sad-stories-5224078

"WHY HUMANS GIVE BIRTH TO HELPLESS BABIES" BY KATE WONG

https://blogs.scientificamerican.com/observations/why-humans-give-birth-to-helpless-babies/

ROMAN TEARS AND THEIR IMPACT: A QUESTION OF GENDER? BY SARAH REY

"A CONSOLATION OF VOICES: AT THE PARK AVENUE ARMORY, MOURNING THE WORLD OVER" BY WILLIAM L. HAMILTON

https://www.nytimes.com/2016/09/12/arts/music/mourning-installation-taryn-simon-park-avenue-armory.html

"I FORGOT HOW TO CRY AS A MAN. HRT GAVE ME A RANGE OF EMOTIONS I NEVER THOUGHT POSSIBLE" BY CADANCE BELL

https://www.theguardian.com/lifeandstyle/2020/jul/20/i-forgot-how-to-cry-as-a-man-hrt-gave-me-a-range-of-emotions-i-never-thought-possible

"14 BENEFITS OF CRYING WHEN YOU NEED TO JUST LET IT ALL OUT, ACCORDING TO EXPERTS" BY KORIN MILLER

https://www.womenshealthmag.com/health/a38150358/benefits-of-crying/

"IS CRYING GOOD FOR YOU?" BY LEO NEWHOUSE

https://www.health.harvard.edu/blog/is-crying-good-for-you-2021030122020

"HOW CRYING COULD ACTUALLY BOOST YOUR MOOD" BY SANCHARI SINHA DUTTA

https://www.news-medical.net/health/How-Crying-Could-Actually-Boost-Your-Mood.aspx

"LA LLORONA: THE STORY OF THE MEXICAN MYTH" BY SILVIA I. MUNGUIA

https://owlcation.com/humanities/La-Llorona-A-Mythical-Figure-of-Mexican-Culture

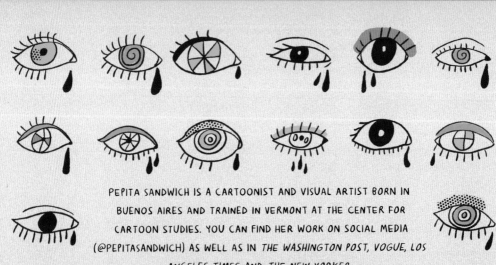

PEPITA SANDWICH IS A CARTOONIST AND VISUAL ARTIST BORN IN
BUENOS AIRES AND TRAINED IN VERMONT AT THE CENTER FOR
CARTOON STUDIES. YOU CAN FIND HER WORK ON SOCIAL MEDIA
(@PEPITASANDWICH) AS WELL AS IN *THE WASHINGTON POST*, *VOGUE*, *LOS
ANGELES TIMES*, AND *THE NEW YORKER*.
HER FIRST TWO BOOKS, *DIARIO DE SUPERVIVENCIA* (SURVIVAL DIARIES,
2016) AND *LAS MUJERES MUEVEN MONTAÑAS* (WOMEN MOVE
MOUNTAINS, 2019), WERE PUBLISHED IN SPANISH. SHE ALSO TEACHES DIARY
COMICS AND VISUAL STORYTELLING. SHE LIVES IN NEW YORK CITY.